Driving
Abroad

SKILLS • ADVICE • SAFETY • LAWS

This book is published in association with the Institute of Advanced Motorists (IAM). The 'World of Motoring' entries throughout have been kindly provided by IAM members, whose names are credited with each entry.

© Robert Davies, 2004

First published April 2001
Reprinted September 2001
Reprinted June 2002
Second Edition April 2004
Reprinted May 2006
Reprinted November 2007
Third Edition February 2009

Every effort has been made to ensure the accuracy of the information given but the author and the publisher accept no responsibility for any injury, loss or inconvenience sustained by anyone using this guide. If you have any comments, information or photographs which would be useful to include in future editions of *Driving Abroad*, please send them to Books Division, Haynes Publishing, Sparkford, Yeovil, Somerset BA22 7JJ.

Haynes Publishing Sparkford, Yeovil, Somerset BA22 7JJ
Telephone: **01963 442030**
Fax: **01963 440001**
E-mail: **sales@haynes.co.uk**
Website: **www.haynes.co.uk**

ISBN 978 1 84425 576 4

British Library Cataloguing in Publication Data
A catalogue record for this book is available from the British Library

Printed by J. H. Haynes & Co. Ltd, Sparkford, Yeovil, Somerset BA22 7JJ, UK

Driving
Abroad

SKILLS • ADVICE • SAFETY • LAWS

THIRD EDITION
ROBERT DAVIES

PUBLISHED IN ASSOCIATION
WITH THE INSTITUTE OF
ADVANCED MOTORISTS

CONTENTS

Driving in Southern Europe — **166**

Driving in Eastern Europe — **182**

Driving in North America — **194**

Driving in Australasia — **202**

Driving in South Africa — **210**

Driving further afield — **214**

DRIVING
ABROAD

British motorists have always enjoyed taking their cars abroad, but since the opening of the Channel Tunnel the number of drivers heading for mainland Europe has soared. Over three million drivers now take their cars to Europe each year – that's about one in seven British motorists.

Millions more hire a car when they fly to a holiday destination. Having your own transport opens up a whole new way to experience a country, giving the freedom to explore exactly where you want, when you want.

7

Why drive abroad?

At a time when driving is increasingly seen as a chore, a frustrating and tedious means of getting from one place to another, driving abroad is a great way to put the fun back into motoring.

Driving along the tree-lined avenues of France, stopping at chateaux and vineyards; chasing the setting sun across the boundless Australian outback; switchbacking between clear sky and crashing surf on America's west coast; or simply hiring a scruffy runaround to search out secluded beaches on a Greek island. These are what classic holiday memories are made of.

Having your own transport opens up endless new possibilities when exploring another country

Since the opening of the Channel Tunnel and Le Shuttle service to France, many more British drivers have started taking their cars abroad

Challenges

But carefree driving abroad requires forethought, preparation and planning. Driving in Nice, Orlando or Sydney is very different to driving in your home town and presents challenges for the most experienced drivers.

In most foreign countries you're required to break the habit of a lifetime's motoring and drive on the right-hand side of the road. Unfamiliar signs have to be interpreted and confusing road layouts tackled. If you've hired a car, you have to adapt to unfamiliar controls and the strange sensation of changing gear with the wrong hand. And you have to learn to cope with local drivers, who won't necessarily react in the way you expect, but in the nature of drivers the world over will be impatient to get to where they are going with little sympathy to spare for a hesitant foreigner.

Preparation

Pitfalls lie in wait for the unwary motorist abroad. Fail to do your paperwork properly, and you could find yourself uninsured if you have an accident, or stranded if you break down miles from nowhere. Drive in ignorance of local motoring laws and you are heading for an embarrassing and potentially expensive encounter with the police. At worst, misunderstanding local driving rules and customs can result in a crash, an upsetting and potentially tragic conclusion to a trip abroad.

DRIVING **ABROAD**

Confidence

The aim of this book is to help you acquire the skills and knowledge needed to tackle the challenge of driving abroad with confidence. Within these pages you'll find advice on what documents you need, how traffic rules vary, how to drive on the 'wrong' side of the road, warnings of unusual road hazards, tips for staying on the right side of the law and advice on what to do if you run into trouble.

Not only should this help you stay safe and legal abroad, it will give you the peace of mind that comes with being properly prepared to meet unfamiliar conditions. And the less you have to worry about running into trouble on the road, the more you can concentrate on appreciating the country you're in.

Drive safely – and enjoy your driving.

World of motoring

Why do we Brits drive on the left when the rest of Europe keeps to the right? Most people are right-handed, and in mediaeval times would have carried their sword on their right – which meant they would rather pass to the left of approaching strangers to keep their sword arm handy in case of trouble. Napoleon, who was left-handed, reversed this tradition after becoming Emperor of France – and continental motorists have kept to the right ever since

Unfamiliar signs, road markings and driving habits, plus the need to drive on the right, make driving abroad a challenge that must be taken seriously to stay out of trouble

ON THE ROAD

We all have vivid memories of our first miles behind the wheel of a car as a learner driver. Simple actions like gear changing or even keeping the car in a straight line needed real concentration to avoid a groan of protest from the gearbox or a cry of alarm from the instructor. That first session of driving probably left you feeling drained out of all proportion to the physical effort expended.

Driving overseas for the first time can feel every bit as disconcerting as that very first time you sat behind the wheel. You have to actively concentrate to stay on the right side of the road. Drivers come at you from unfamiliar directions, they don't signal as you expect and they overtake where you don't expect. Even stopping at a filling station to top up your tank can be a confusing experience.

It takes a while to adjust, and until you do you will find that the extra concentration required is tiring. But the better prepared you are, the quicker and easier you'll adapt to driving abroad.

11

The first day driving abroad is always the most difficult, so avoid busy towns and crowded roads until you acclimatise

Road casualties worldwide

Deaths annually per 10,000 motor vehicles

Norway	1.1
Switzerland	1.4
UK	1.5
Australia	1.8
Germany	1.9
United States	2.0
New Zealand	2.2
France	2.6
Spain	2.9
Ireland	3.4
Portugal	4.8
Thailand	9.0
South Africa	17.0
India	20.0
Venezuela	58.0
Kenya	64.0

Road safety

If asked about the dangers of going abroad, many people mention the fear of being in a plane crash. Others worry about being mugged, or falling prey to a nasty tropical disease. Few appreciate that the biggest risk they run abroad is being involved in a road crash.

Driving is dangerous, but it's a danger that society as a whole is strangely prepared to tolerate. A rail crash is met with outrage and demands for action, while the ceaseless toll of death on the road continues with rarely a mention on our TV screens.

Every year there are some 300,000 road casualties in the UK. And yet this country is actually one of the safest places in the world in which to drive. You might not think it when you're on the M25 in the rush hour, but by global standards, British drivers are disciplined, well behaved and courteous.

Hop over the Channel to France and the chance of meeting with a fatal crash on the road almost doubles. France has 2.6 deaths each year for every 10,000 motor vehicles on its roads, compared with 1.5 in the UK.

In popular holiday destinations such as Greece or Portugal, the risk of dying in a car crash is about four times higher than in the UK. The more exotic the location, the worse the figures seem to be. Thailand, for instance, has 9.0 deaths per 10,000 motor vehicles, and South Africa has 17. In parts of the developing world – where you would be best advised not to even think about driving – death rates are appalling, reaching over 100 per 10,000 motor vehicles.

ON THE ROAD

Safe driving

Road casualty statistics can be frightening, but there's no need to panic. We refer to car crashes as road accidents, but in fact there's nothing accidental about the vast majority of them. Most crashes are caused by bad driving. But no matter how bad the driving around you may be, you are in control of your own vehicle and by driving safely and defensively you can minimise the danger wherever you are.

When you drive in another country for the first time, many things are strange. You may be behind the wheel of an unfamiliar left-hand-drive car. Road markings, traffic lights, speed limits and sign posts all look different, and even the drivers may not do what you'd expect them to do back home.

But these basic rules of safe driving hold true, whether you are in Manchester or Marseilles, London or Los Angeles:

• **Read the road:** the further ahead you look, the more time you give yourself to recognise and respond to potential road hazards. When abroad signs and road layouts can be confusing so you need to identify them early and if necessary change your position to get into the right lane. Keep an eye on everything that's happening around you. In heavy traffic it's easy to become mesmerised by the tailgate of the car in front, but you should keep looking well ahead of it as well as monitoring what's happening in your mirrors.

• **Anticipate:** drivers often pride themselves on their quick reactions but the really good driver anticipates the problem that's coming, slows down well in

World of motoring

"I recently drove from Vienna to Budapest and was delighted to find some simple, effective, and helpful road markings. These were horizontal stripes across the carriageway at precise intervals (presumably calculated for speeds of 100kph). Alongside was the simple message: 'Two bars – too close'. These were repeated every few miles and I found it easy to gauge the distance between vehicles using this system. Wouldn't it be fun to see it on the M25 during morning rush hour?"
Des Lyver

Leaving plenty of space in front of your car gives you more time to react if anything goes wrong on the road ahead

Driving abroad can be a carefree and enjoyable way to spend a holiday, but you must never forget your responsibility to ensure the safety of yourself, your passengers and other road users

advance and so doesn't need to take emergency action to avoid it. For example, when following a bus, anticipate when it's likely to halt at a bus stop, hang back and give yourself space to overtake smoothly. At a roundabout, slow down well in advance instead of braking at the last moment so you give following drivers more time to react to your actions. Approaching a motorway junction, anticipate that other drivers may swing across in front of you as they attempt to exit and leave space for them to do so.

• **Create space:** the more space there is around your vehicle, the more time you have to react if anything goes wrong and the more chance you have of finding an escape route. Many drivers travel too close to the car in front. If it brakes unexpectedly, they have no safety zone. If they do manage to carry out an emergency stop without hitting the car in front, a following car may plough into their rear. Always leave at least a two-second gap between yourself and the car in front – and double this in poor weather. If another car moves into the gap, ease back and open up a safe space again.

• **Assume the worst:** never assume that another driver has seen you or will react as you expect. Other drivers may be half asleep, distracted, careless or even drunk. In a foreign country, they may deal with a given driving situation quite differently to the way you would expect drivers to react back home. Give them (and yourself) space to make mistakes and never rely on someone else's reactions to keep you safe when making a manoeuvre like merging into a stream of traffic.

• **Concentrate:** at 70mph a car covers more than 100ft every second. Looking away at a critical moment could be disastrous. Driving demands high concentration, never more so than when driving abroad when so much is unfamiliar. Don't try to drive when your concentration levels are low, such as when you're tired after stepping off a long-haul flight, or when you are feeling unwell.

Preparing your car

If you usually cover 100 miles a week around town, then expecting your car to cope with a 2,000-mile dash across Europe is asking for trouble. Get it checked and given a clean bill of health before you leave.

Look up when the next service is due, and if there's any chance that your mileage while abroad will exceed the next service interval than have the car serviced before you depart.

Make sure there is plenty of tread left on your tyres. The UK legal limit of 1.6mm across the central three-quarters of the tyre is an absolute minimum and you should replace any tyre with less than 3mm of tread across the whole width before embarking on a lengthy European trip. Ensure that the spare tyre is in good condition too, and that you have a wheel brace and jack in case you need to replace it. Check that all tyres are inflated to the correct pressure.

Ensure that oil and coolant levels are correct. Fill up the screenwash; if you're heading to alpine regions in winter both screenwash and engine coolant solutions need to be strong enough to cope with temperatures as low as –30C.

A tool kit is handy to have on board, although what you pack may depend on your mechanical ability. It can also pay to take items which are a common cause of breakdowns, such as an alternator belt and clutch and accelerator cables. Even if you can't fit these yourself, they may save you time waiting for parts to be sourced locally. Don't forget to take a spare set of keys with you too.

Maintenance

If you are covering a high mileage you'll need to keep a watchful eye on your car during the trip.

Daily: carry out a visual inspection of the tyres and check windscreen and lights for damage. Clean lights and windscreen in bad weather.

Weekly: check oil and windscreen washer level and tyre pressures (when tyres are cold). Ensure all lights are working, including brake lights.

Check tyre pressures at least once a week – but make sure you do this before you start driving, when the tyres are cold, or you may get an inaccurate reading

Right or left?

We may be outnumbered by European countries driving on the right, but Britain is by no means the only place where drivers still stick to the left. Other left-hand-drivers include:

Australia
Cyprus
India
Japan
Kenya
Malaysia
Malta
Mauritius
Mozambique
Namibia
South Africa
Tanzania
Thailand
New Zealand

World of motoring

"It's helpful to know that in the US they paint a white line on the right-hand side of the carriageway and a yellow line on the centre or left-hand side. So if you remember 'White on the right, yellow on the left,' you'll be going the right way."
David Gray

Driving on the right

Driving on the 'wrong' side of the road is the single most worrying aspect of going abroad for most British motorists. Keeping left is ingrained in us from the first day we get behind the wheel so the prospect of doing everything back to front can be daunting.

Fortunately, most drivers find that making the switch turns out to be easier than they expect. Once you enter the traffic flow there are many visual cues, including the positioning of other vehicles, directional signs and road markings, which help to keep you on the right track.

The first day of driving on the right is always the most difficult, particularly as you may already be weary after a tiring flight or ferry crossing. If possible, keep your driving to a minimum, have an early night and start out when you're refreshed and able to concentrate fully the next morning.

Make life easier for yourself by steering clear of tricky situations in the early stages of driving abroad too. Heading straight into a city centre before you've given yourself a chance to acclimatise is asking for trouble. Trying to cope with both the new sensation of driving on the right and the bombardment of hazards in busy town traffic can quickly overload the senses.

The easiest way to acclimatise to driving abroad is to cover your first kilometres on the motorway. Here there are fewer distractions, no traffic heading at you from unexpected directions, and junctions and hazards are clearly signposted.

Although it's relatively easy to remember to drive on the right when in a stream of traffic, there are certain situations when you are more likely to be caught out. Be especially careful when rejoining a road from a lay-by or petrol station. It's all too easy to swing out without thinking on to the wrong side of the road.

This particularly applies in the quiet of the countryside, when about to drive back on to the road after stopping for a picnic or to admire the

ON THE ROAD

view. If there are no other vehicles on the road, there are few clues in the form of signs or road markings to remind you to drive on the right.

Another situation which requires caution is driving on a narrow road which doesn't have a central white line. When you meet oncoming traffic and have to pull over, the habit of a lifetime can take over and cause you to steer to the left – potentially into a head-on crash.

These sorts of mistakes are particularly easy to make a week or more into a driving holiday. You've become so used to driving on the right that you may no longer be concentrating so hard, and a momentary lapse can easily occur.

To avoid these sort of situations, it can be useful to repeat to yourself the mantra 'Think Right – Look Left'. Do this every time you pull out on to the road, and at all those moments when your mind goes blank or you have a few seconds of panic because you have become disorientated.

Saying 'Think Right – Look Left' puts you in the right place on the road and travelling in the direction of the traffic flow. It will also get you looking in the direction from where the first danger is most likely to come.

Try taping this mantra on your steering wheel, or ask your passengers to remind you to keep right whenever you set off. You could make this a game for the kids – and it may turn out to be a lifesaver.

World of motoring
"The first day of any trip abroad has a driver's full concentration to avoid driving on the wrong side. The danger comes in a day or two, perhaps pulling out after an overnight stop when there is no traffic about. Yes, I have done it, in Germany once after a refuelling stop, but fortunately I quickly realised my mistake. As a reminder, I now put a length of white tape on the steering wheel hub as soon as I arrive on the continent. It reminds me every time I get into the driving seat."
Derek Eastell

When pulling back onto the road from a lay-by or filling station, extra care is needed as it's easy to forget that you're meant to be driving on the right-hand side of the road

Taking your own car abroad brings the added complication of driving a right-hand-drive car on the right. Extra care is needed when positioning the car on the road to compensate for your restricted vision

Overtaking needs special care abroad. Pay attention to no-overtaking signs (above) and road markings. Many countries use a single solid white line to prohibit overtaking in both directions, unlike the double solid white line we have in the UK

Right-hand-drive cars

If you're taking your own car abroad, you face the added complication of driving a right-hand-drive car on the wrong side of the road. Just as when driving a left-hand-drive car in the UK, you need to take this into account when positioning your car on the road. Remember that when pulling up at tolls or car park entrances, you'll be sitting on the wrong side of the car to collect a ticket, so delegate this job to your passenger.

Readjust your rear view mirrors to get the best view of following traffic. Your left-hand mirror will become more important when joining motorways and checking for overtaking traffic, so make sure it is clean and properly adjusted.

Overtaking

One manoeuvre which becomes especially difficult in a right-hand-drive car abroad is overtaking. Your view forward may be obscured by the vehicle in front so compensate by pulling back from it to increase your field of vision. Make use of opportunities to view the road ahead along the inside of the vehicle in front. Be cautious about asking a passenger to tell you when it is safe to overtake, especially if they are not a qualified driver. It's your decision, so even if a passenger gives you the go-ahead, pull out to get a full view of the road ahead but do not commit to overtaking without being certain that it is safe to do so.

Because of your restricted vision, while preparing to overtake you may appear hesitant to following traffic, so make full use of your left-hand mirror to check that no-one is about to try passing you just as you pull out, and give plenty of warning with your indicator.

In some countries, such as Sweden and Ireland, main roads have a white line painted along their nearside to form a hard shoulder. Slower moving vehicles move over on to this hard shoulder to let following traffic overtake. If a vehicle in front of you pulls over, don't accept this as an invitation to overtake without first checking that it is completely safe to do so. There may be junctions or obstructions on the hard shoulder that could cause the vehicle being overtaken to suddenly pull back on to the main carriageway. Similarly, when you want to let another vehicle pass, pull over only when there is a safe clear stretch of road ahead.

It's usual to flash headlights or sound the horn before overtaking in some countries, so if a driver does this to you don't assume he's being impatient. In Luxembourg it's compulsory to flash before overtaking when outside a built-up area at night.

Undertaking
In Britain, and most of the rest of the world, undertaking – or overtaking on the inside lane – is illegal on motorways and dual carriageways unless traffic is forming a queue in the outside lane.

In America a quite different rule applies and undertaking is permitted on multi-lane highways. Strictly speaking drivers are meant to keep to the inside lane when not overtaking but in practice few seem to do this. Many stay in a middle lane to avoid being siphoned off when the inner lane becomes a compulsory exit lane at a junction.

Drivers used to the British system must take extra care when pulling into a nearside lane that nothing is passing in that lane unexpectedly. Also be aware that traffic crossing the road to join a dual carriageway will generally enter the outside lane and stay there, expecting you to go past on the inside lane.

World of motoring
"In Slovenia, on non-motorway roads where there is a hard shoulder, it is common practice for slower vehicles to pull over and drive on the hard shoulder to let other vehicles overtake when it is safe to do so (though there is a strong tendency for drivers to overtake anyway, even when it is decidedly unsafe.)"
Harry Wilby

Not all drivers bother to signal before changing lanes, so aim to anticipate when a vehicle ahead is about to make a manoeuvre and leave plenty of space for it

World of motoring
"In California, indicators must be used whenever pulling away from the kerb, changing lanes or turning, even if there's nobody about. But this is universally ignored. In fact, indicator use is so infrequent, that in the rare cases when they are used, they are usually left on for the next five miles or so."
Rod Duggan

Signalling
Using indicators to give other road users a clear advance warning when you intend to turn or change your position on the road is vital for safe driving. When driving abroad you may be slow to negotiate unfamiliar hazards or junctions, so it is especially important to give other traffic a clear indication of what you intend to do. Remember, though, that you should never assume other drivers will notice your signal, understand it or react to it as you expect.

Although they serve such a useful purpose, indicators are often misused, and many drivers use their indicator without thinking about the purpose it should be serving. It's all too common to see drivers indicate after they have begun to change lane, too late for it to serve any useful function. Always use indicators well in advance of the manoeuvre to give other road users a chance to react.

In some countries – such as Germany – drivers tend to be better disciplined in using their indicators than we are in the UK. In others, particularly the United States, drivers often don't bother indicating at all. Always be extremely cautious when following a car that slows down – it may be about to make a turn without warning.

When we're taught to drive in the UK, we're told to signal only where it serves a useful purpose for other road users – for instance, signalling after overtaking is not recommended, as it's obvious a car has to pull back to its side of the road after overtaking. Not all countries share this view, however, so it's best to follow local practice. In a few countries it's actually a legal requirement to signal when returning to your side of the road after overtaking.

Headlamp flash
Picture the scene. The road narrows over a bridge, leaving a space only wide enough for one vehicle. An oncoming car is approaching from the other side and flashes its headlamps at you. What do you do?

In England most drivers would assume the signal

means 'come through, I'm giving way'. But to most French drivers it means just the opposite: 'Give way, I'm coming through'. It follows that you should never assume that a driver flashing headlamps is indicating that it is safe for you to go. When someone does flash, wait and make certain of their intentions before moving.

A headlamp flash has only one meaning you can be certain of, which is to alert other road users to your presence. Use it and interpret it as this wherever you are driving.

Horn use

In Britain we don't use the horn much, but in some other countries it seems drivers can't get enough of it. Many Third World roads reverberate to the sound of continual honking, while in Southern Europe sitting at a junction half a second after the lights have changed can incite a fanfare of horns behind you.

Actually, a lot of foreign drivers use their horns more sensibly than we do. There's a feeling in the UK that honking at another driver is rather rude. This means that the horn sometimes doesn't get used when it would be a positive safety benefit – for example, to alert the driver in front that you're about to overtake. This sort of sensible horn use is much more common in many other European countries.

When abroad you might be tempted to join in with the local horn chorus but don't get carried away. Many countries are getting sick of the sound of incessant honking and are cracking down on excessive horn use. There are often regulations prohibiting use of the horn when stationary or in built-up areas at night.

Never use your horn to reprimand another road user who you consider has done something wrong. This serves no purpose and is exactly the sort of gesture than can cause road rage incidents. In other countries, just as in the UK, the horn has one purpose and one purpose only: to warn other road users that you are there.

Regulations often prohibit horn use in certain areas or at specific times, so take care to obey a no-horn sign if you come across one – even if local drivers seem to ignore it

Busy road junctions abroad can be confusing. Remember that in most other countries, traffic joining from the right automatically has right of way unless signs or road markings direct otherwise

Right of way

In many countries drivers must give way to traffic coming from the right unless there is an indication to the contrary. So if you're driving through a French village, a driver may be quite entitled to pull out of a side street on your right expecting you to give way.

This rule can easily catch out British drivers so be prepared to give way to the right unless signs specifically show you have right of way.

A yellow diamond sign indicates you are on a road which has right of way over roads joining it, and this is posted on most main roads across the Continent. Where you see the yellow diamond crossed out it means you no longer have right of way, so be cautious.

Motorways

Motorways provide the quickest, safest and most convenient means of covering long distances. For anyone new to driving in an unfamiliar country, they offer a relatively easy introduction to driving on the other side of the road. Traffic is all heading in the same direction, at a similar speed, and signs are usually clear and well posted.

A yellow diamond sign means that the road you are on has priority over all roads joining it. When this sign is cancelled (below) you must be prepared to give way to traffic joining from the right, even from a minor road

The good news for British drivers heading across the Channel is that Europe has a comprehensive, well-maintained motorway network. Most other European countries have more motorways than we do (Germany, for instance, has more than twice as many motorway miles for its area than the UK). This means that outside obvious congestion hot spots, such as commuter rush hours near cities, and the end of holiday weekends on routes heading back to town, drivers used to the nose-to-tail frustration of the M1, M6 or M25 should be pleasantly surprised by the light traffic on European motorways.

The bad news is that you will probably have to pay for the privilege of using the motorway. Many European motorways are toll roads (called *péage* in France) and they can add considerably to the cost of a long journey.

ON THE ROAD

Some countries, such as Austria and Switzerland, don't impose tolls on individual motorway trips but operate a blanket tax. You must purchase a tax disc called a *vignette* and display it on your windscreen before using the motorway system.

Be alert for features you may not be used to on British motorways. Signposting may not be given as far in advance as on British motorways, so get into the right lane in plenty of time to take your turning. Be prepared to slow down more rapidly on exiting the motorway, as slip roads can have surprisingly tight curves. Take note of the speed limit for the exit road which is sometimes posted where it leaves the motorway.

High-speed driving

Several European countries have a higher motorway speed limit than Britain's 70mph. In France and Austria the limit is 130km/h (81mph). Italy has recently raised the limit on some of its motorways to 150km/h (93mph). Certain sections of German *Autobahn* famously have no speed limit at all, although a limit of 130km/h is recommended.

Whatever the legal limit, don't be tempted to drive too fast. Set a pace that is both legal and comfortable. Pressing on may save a few minutes but over a long distance the extra concentration needed can leave you feeling drained, and fuel economy will suffer too.

World of motoring
"Some motorways in Germany and Poland are in a dangerous state for motorcyclists. So many heavy lorries use them that two parallel wheel grooves are left sunk into the road surface and your wheels get stuck in the ruts. Next year I will travel more on the scenic routes."
Jim Fairclough

Take care to get into the right lane well in advance when approaching a busy motorway junction. In America the inside lane often becomes a compulsory exit lane

German drivers may routinely cruise at over 100mph on the Autobahn, but driving at such high speeds demands a lot of skill and concentration

World of motoring

"German drivers use their main beam on the Autobahn to indicate they would really like the outside lane free for them. If it is not, they tend to use their indicators to ask you to move over and let them by. This also applies if you are in the middle lane. A car close behind may be signalling but does not change lane. He may mean that he cannot move into the outside lane because of approaching traffic and is requesting that you allow him to pass, by changing lane yourself."
David Clarke

It is tempting when reaching a stretch of unrestricted Autobahn to take the opportunity to drive at far higher speeds than are legal in the UK. The best advice is to stick to the recommended 130km/h, but if you do intend exceeding this, bear in mind the following:

♦ Although they permit high speeds, many stretches of Autobahn are intrinsically less safe than equivalent British motorways. They often have only two lanes in each direction and feature sharp bends which can be alarming at speed.

♦ The distance you need to stop increases dramatically with speed. From 70mph it takes at least 75 metres to come to a halt, but at 120mph that stretches to a minimum of 220 metres – and that's ignoring the time it takes to react first.

♦ Local drivers who are storming by in their Porsches and Mercedes may have years of experience of driving at these speeds which helps them to make the necessary mental adjustments. Germans also tend to be unusually well disciplined behind the wheel.

♦ Speed limits may be lowered at night, or in wet weather. Limits apply at roadworks, and these may be strictly monitored by speed cameras.

♦ If you are going to drive at high speed you must consult your car's handbook and set your tyre pressures to the recommended limit. Most recommend setting a higher pressure for high-speed driving.

♦ Do not drive at high speed if you have any doubts about the mechanical health of your car. High speed subjects a car to a lot more stress than usual. It may expose faults within the engine, brakes or cooling system that have gone unnoticed at normal speeds.

♦ After driving at high speed, keep a close eye on your speedometer when you leave the motorway. It will take time for you to adjust to driving at a lower speed.

ON THE ROAD

A need for speed

Options for drivers wishing to drive legally at high speed elsewhere in the globe are fast running out. In the US, Montana decided to scrap its freeway speed limit in 1995, achieving brief notoriety and the nickname 'Montanabahn'. But the state has since reversed this decision and introduced a 75mph limit.

The Northern Territory of Australia is one other place with no maximum speed limit on its major road artery, the Stuart Highway (known locally as *The Track*), which carves an arrow straight course across the outback to Alice Springs. As you go long stretches without even meeting another vehicle this leads to fewer accidents than would be expected in more populous regions, although drivers should bear in mind the potentially fatal consequences of hitting a kangaroo at high speed.

Driving cultures

Italians drive too fast. Germans like big cars. Scandinavians would never dream of breaking the speed limit. We all have preconceptions about foreign drivers and some of them even turn out to be true.

Different cultures have very different attitudes to driving. In Greece, three times as many drivers say they routinely drive through amber traffic lights than drivers in the UK. In one survey, three-quarters of Italian drivers felt that motorists should be free to decide for themselves how much they can drink before driving; in Sweden only one-fifth of drivers felt the same way.

Anyone who has driven in southern Europe will know that drivers there place more emphasis on making fast progress than we do in the UK. Some visitors find this intimidating and unnerving, others may find the faster driving style exhilarating. But ultimately, there's no doubt that it is less safe. Drivers run three times the risk of meeting their death on the road in Portugal or Greece than in the UK.

To avoid becoming one of these statistics, you need to adapt your driving style to take into account local

World of motoring

"In the course of a three-month trip I hired vehicles to drive from San Francisco to Los Angeles, around the South and North Islands of New Zealand, and from Sydney to Brisbane in Australia. If anyone wonders if driving outside the UK can be hairy – forget it. The patience, tolerance and lane discipline I experienced were amazing. On landing at Heathrow a friend drove me down the M3 to Basingstoke and the antics on this stretch of motorway surpassed anything I had seen in LA or any other conurbation I had visited."
Ken Walsh

Driving in some Southern European countries can feel chaotic at times. Much concentration may be needed to cope with the pace of local traffic

World of motoring
Mind your manners when driving in Germany. Making rude gestures or swearing at other motorists is illegal there and could earn you a hefty fine

habits. Drivers may overtake more often and in situations where you might not expect them to. Every time you round a blind bend, be prepared to encounter oncoming drivers exploiting what would be considered a decidedly marginal overtaking opportunity back home.

Where fast driving is the norm drivers may expect you not to impede their progress. A car will overtake on a two-lane road, expecting oncoming vehicles to move towards the verge and make room for it to squeeze through. In most cases other drivers co-operate with none of the honking or fist-waving which might follow a similar manoeuvre in Britain.

In fact there's a refreshing absence of the attitude so often seen in the UK, which seems to say 'I'm driving quite fast enough so why should I let you overtake' and leads to some drivers forming conga-like queues behind them. When they see you in their rear view mirror, drivers in southern Europe are more likely to help you overtake, by pulling to the side of the road and using their nearside indicator to show they're letting you pass. Always be certain in your own mind that it's safe to overtake before doing so.

Return the compliment and give following drivers the opportunity to overtake when it arises. If you want to drive at a leisurely pace and admire the scenery, you'll enjoy it much more without the distraction of a car up your rear bumper.

Driving styles in some countries can seem rude and aggressive to British eyes. High-speed tailgating on the motorway is a particularly unnerving habit in Italy, especially when you don't have a clear lane to move into. In Germany, drivers will flash to clear the road ahead in a way that might seem arrogant, while in French cities you're allowed no time to take your bearings at road junctions before someone hoots at you to get a move on.

Keep calm in these situations. Behaviour that might seem rude in ours eyes may be perfectly acceptable in other cultures. Don't be obstructive or give other drivers a ticking off by honking, flashing or gesticulating at them. Trying to change other drivers' habits is a fruitless exercise at home, let alone when you're abroad. The only driver whose behaviour you have any control over is your own.

In some areas, particularly southern Europe, drivers can also exhibit an elastic approach to motoring law. Speed limits seem universally ignored, and parking regulations flouted. But don't be tempted to follow their example. Local drivers may know just when, where and how far the law can be stretched; it's much easier for a foreigner to be caught out.

Not all driving cultures seem fast and aggressive to British eyes. In Scandinavia, you may need to attune yourself to making slower progress in a land of lower speed limits and law-abiding drivers. In some countries, driving styles are more laid back than in Britain. This is often so in countrified areas, especially in rural America. When visiting such places, remember that the driving tactics needed to navigate the M25 each morning might seem unpleasantly pushy and aggressive to local drivers.

World of motoring

"In Norway courtesy is constant on the roads, even one memorable evening in Tromsø when my son elected to instruct the locals in the art of driving on the left, choosing the only set of traffic lights in town. Not a gasp, gesture or hoot as the traffic divided and gently flowed around us."
Fiona Haig

No matter what the provocation, this sort of angry response is never justified – especially abroad where the etiquette on the road may be very different to what we're used to at home

Just because you have a car doesn't mean you have to drive every day. Using public transport makes an interesting change, especially in places like Switzerland where it is both efficient and convenient

Public transport

A driving holiday is a great way to explore a country but sometimes you can return feeling you've seen an awful lot but not had a great deal of time to unwind.

Remember that just because you have your car with you, you don't have to use it every day. Schedule some rest days when you leave the car behind for the day. Using public transport instead can give you a whole different insight into local life, and it lets you relax and spend lunchtime in the local bar instead of confining yourself to Perrier.

Ditch the car as soon as you can when heading into a big city. Cities can be a nightmare to negotiate by car. A growing number operate zones in which car access is restricted and parking spaces may be hard to find and expensive. Stop at a secure car park on the edge of town, get a bus or train to the centre and you'll have a far more enjoyable time.

Avoiding fatigue

Tiredness kills. In fact, as more research is carried out on the causes of road accidents, the more it's being recognised that driver fatigue is a serious problem. As many as one in five motorway accidents are caused by drivers falling asleep at the wheel. And crashes caused by a sleepy driver tend to be bad ones because the driver is unable to slow down or take avoiding action.

Drivers going abroad are vulnerable to fatigue, particularly when trying to push themselves to cover long distances rapidly. It's tempting to drive into the night to put some miles under the wheels, but you need to be cautious about trying to keep going when your body thinks it should be in bed. Accidents are particularly likely when the body's rhythms are in a natural trough, in the early hours of the morning and just after lunch when many sensible Continentals are taking a siesta.

It's vital to avoid taking medicines that cause drowsiness as a side-effect. Anti-motion sickness pills, sedative antihistamines and certain cold and flu remedies are among drugs available over the counter which can make driving dangerous. Be particularly careful when purchasing drugs overseas which may not carry a clear warning that they can cause drowsiness.

Plan your journey to take sufficient breaks. A minimum break of at least 15 minutes after every two hours driving is recommended. In France make full use of the excellent system of rest stops (called *aires de repos*) that are situated at frequent intervals along the autoroutes. Rest areas on American freeways and in Australia and New Zealand often have historical plaques giving a snippet of information about the area you're passing through, and these can enhance the interest of a journey, particularly when you have children on board.

Don't set over-optimistic targets for the distances you plan to cover, and remember that driving on the right can be stressful, particularly for the first day, and will tire you more quickly than usual. If possible share the driving and swap drivers before you start to feel tired.

Most importantly, if you start feeling sleepy, stop and take a break. It is not sufficient to open the window or turn up the radio. The best way to counteract drowsiness is to pull off the road, drink some strong coffee (a double espresso is ideal), then wind back the car seat and take a 15-minute nap. The caffeine in the coffee won't stop you going to sleep, as it takes half an hour or so to kick in, but when you do wake you should feel fresher and able to continue your journey.

Fatigue is a potential killer, but drivers usually get plenty of warning that they are getting tired. Heed the signs when this happens, pull off the road and take a break

Contented children are the secret to a happy family holiday – so take along plenty of toys, games and sweets to combat the monotony of a long drive

Keeping children amused

Children and long car journeys are a fraught combination. Children get bored and irritable, and squabbling can be a real distraction for the driver. In one motoring survey nine out of ten parents admitted being distracted by their children while at the wheel, and one in fourteen had been involved in an accident as a result.

So be sure to take along plenty of crayons and colouring books, tapes and toys to keep them amused. Older children may appreciate simple language tapes for the country you're heading for. A retractable sun blind or two can be a good idea to keep out the Mediterranean heat.

Frequent breaks are vital, for the driver as well as the children, but when you have a long distance to cover, don't make the breaks too much fun. If the break is more interesting than the journey, the children will soon be clamouring to stop again once you're back on the road. Let them eat and drink in the car rather than during the break. Just as in an aircraft, eating helps break up the monotony of long-distance travel.

Travel sickness

Nothing makes a long journey more miserable for a child than travel sickness. Properly called motion sickness, it's caused when the jiggling motion of car travel upsets the organ of balance in the inner ear. Other factors can exacerbate the condition, including poor ventilation, a full stomach or the sight of food.

Sufferers should try to focus on the horizon outside the car rather than trying to concentrate on reading or playing a game inside. For persistent cases, remedies are available from the chemist, some of which are taken orally before the journey, others are administered as an adhesive patch worn on the skin.

ON THE ROAD

Route planning

Navigating in other countries can be confusing. Signs may be less conspicuous or not placed where you expect, destination names unfamiliar, and there may be complex interchanges where it's easy to take a wrong turning.

Direction signs can be confusing when they give only the name of an obscure town on the main road heading to a larger city, or just give the road number with no place name. In French towns, follow the signs marked *Toutes Directions* – they'll take you out of town to where you'll find signposts for wherever you're heading.

Thorough route planning is essential to minimise the chances of going wrong. Make sure you possess

World of motoring
"In the US it is wise to have a good map and a very clear idea of which direction you are heading. Interstate highways apart, there are very few named directions and you are likely to arrive at a junction which simply states *Vermont 100 North-South*."
Beryl Dean

In countries such as America, route signs are more likely to give road numbers than destinations, which makes a map vital

Speedometers in UK cars must be clearly marked with kilometres as well as miles per hour. A speed of 100kph is roughly equivalent to 60mph

World of motoring

The wealthy and famous are taking to the air to beat traffic jams on the Côte d'Azur. Over 20 helipads have opened around the resort of San Tropez, leading to complaints that the skies – already among the most crowded in Europe – are becoming dangerously congested

a detailed, large-scale map of the country you are driving through. There is a dual system of main route numbering in operation in the EU. In addition to individual country road numbering, the European International Network is based a grid system. Roads are given a number beginning with 'E', with even numbers running east to west and odd numbers north to south. These roads are identified by green and white signs, and can make navigation a lot easier when you are crossing borders. (The UK has signed up to the E-road convention but our E-road network isn't signposted as such.)

There's a similar situation in the US where the national system of Interstate roads can be called something quite different in individual states. American directions generally just give the road number and its direction (north, south, east, west).

Satellite navigation systems are a boon when it comes to finding your way through unknown territory, but make sure you have the right CDs for the country you are visiting. Or visit the website *www.mappy.com*, which will provide you with a detailed itinerary for your route, plus useful extra information such as cost of tolls and an estimate of fuel costs for your journey.

Distances

Most of the world measures distance in kilometres, which can lead to some confusion for British people who still think in miles.

One kilometre is equal to 0.621 miles. If you're happier working with fractions, one method of converting kilometres to miles is to multiply the figure in kilometres by five and then divide the result by eight. Thus 100 kilometres multiplied by five equals 500, which divided by eight equals 62.5 miles.

Another way to achieve a rough conversion is called the six rule. Simply multiply the figure in kilometres by six, then move the decimal point one digit to the left. So 100km multiplied by six equals 600km, move the decimal place to the left and you have 60 miles.

ON THE ROAD

Avoiding congestion

Just as the Bank Holiday traffic jam is a tradition of British motoring life, so drivers heading abroad must expect to encounter congestion at peak periods.

Try to avoid routes heading into and out of major cities at the start and end of the weekend. Expect to meet heavy traffic at the start of the holiday season, particularly during the first two weeks of August, when autoroutes to the south of France can become clogged. Routes leading to the ski slopes can get similarly congested during the alpine season. Tailbacks are likely to form at borders at busy times, particularly heading out of the EU where passport checks are required.

Roadworks, of course, can cause congestion at any time. Details of roadworks in Europe can be found on BBC2 Ceefax.

In-car navigation systems are becoming widely available and are an invaluable aid to finding your way through unfamiliar territory. Additional discs may be needed to use a UK system in Europe

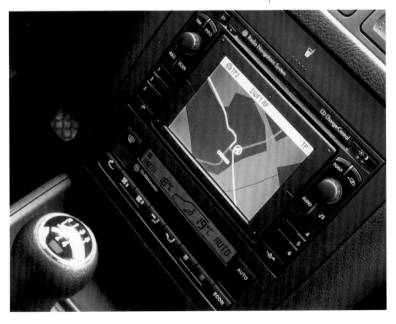

When filling up at a gas station in America you often have to pay the cashier before you start pumping. Petrol there is amazingly cheap, selling at under half the price in the UK

World of motoring
"If you intend to use your credit card to buy fuel in Spain, make sure you have your passport with you. You may find that a petrol station will not accept payment by card without it. Unfortunately, with self-serve you may not discover this until you have already filled your tank."
Les Spedding

Filling up

As in the UK, unleaded petrol is used across the Continent. If uncertain, ask for *Sans Plomb* in France or *Bleifrei* in Germany.

Diesel (*gazole* or *gasoil*) is cheap on the Continent, in many countries costing around a third less than a litre of unleaded.

Leaded petrol has been withdrawn from sale over much of Europe. As in the UK, it is possible to purchase lead replacement petrol (LRP), but not all filling stations stock this so if your car needs it you should carry a bottle of additive which can be put in unleaded when that is all that is available.

Super unleaded or 98 octane petrol (called *Super* in France) can be found across the Continent, although availability may be patchy. Only a few, high performance models need to use this and even they can generally run on normal 95 octane unleaded for short periods without problems. If in doubt consult your manufacturer.

ON THE ROAD

Liquid petroleum gas (LPG) is a popular fuel in some European countries, such as France, Belgium and the Netherlands, where it is readily available at filling stations. Sites in Germany are slightly fewer, and LPG is not available in Spain. Bear in mind when planning a trip that gas-powered cars are not permitted on Eurotunnel.

You'll find a combination of self-service and attended filling stations abroad. In most countries credit cards are accepted, but always be prepared to resort to cash when off the beaten track.

Drivers heading across the Atlantic to hire a car in America will be pleased to discover how cheap *gas* is, costing under half the price we pay at pumps in the UK. There are three grades of unleaded available at US pumps: 87, 89, and 93 octane. The higher octane grades are aimed at high performance models and most cars are quite happy with the cheapest grade – but it's worth confirming this when you hire a car.

Inconvenient though it sounds, at a lot of American filling stations you have to pay for your fuel *before* you start pumping. First pay the cashier for the amount you think you'll need, then fill up and the pump will automatically cut out when it has delivered the amount you've paid for. If you overestimate the amount of fuel you need and you fill your tank before you have received the amount of fuel you've bought, you'll need to return to the cashier to get a refund.

Be cautious if a service attendant offers to check your oil and tyres unless you are just starting out for the day. High-speed driving causes tyre pressures to rise and gives an artificially high reading. Similarly, oil needs time to settle after a high-speed run before you can get an accurate dipstick reading.

Don't forget to keep an eye on your oil consumption. It may be higher than usual if you're doing a lot of high-speed motoring, and need regular topping up

ROAD
HAZARDS

Driving at home we take road hazards such as junctions, traffic lights, roundabouts and level crossings in our stride. But when driving abroad it can never be assumed that features like these are used in the way we're used to. Other road users can present some unusual hazards too. There may be many more cyclists, trams and scooters than we're used to seeing on the road back home.

Extra attention has to be paid to warning signs and road markings. These signs may be unfamiliar, and you will need to slow down and give yourself plenty of time to assess a hazard and decide the safest way to approach it.

In many countries there are hazards we simply don't come across in the UK. Even wild animals can pose a threat that must be taken seriously to stay safe on the road abroad.

A sign like this might look comical, but in Australia kangaroos are a serious motoring hazard. Hitting one even at a relatively slow speed can be fatal

38

Traffic signs may be more familiar abroad than you expect. This Spanish 'no right turn' sign will be clear to any British motorist, while the unique inverted triangle shape of the 'give way' sign reveals its meaning whatever language it's written in

World of motoring
"One sign in Norway confused us. We made a literal translation with the aid of a Norwegian dictionary and came up with 'Fairy Grate'. On seeing the sign again we watched carefully for the hazard – it was a cattle grid! I imagine that signs saying 'No Hard Shoulder' on British motorways are equally baffling for foreign visitors."
Howard Prestage

Traffic signs

How will I understand foreign traffic signs? That's a question many motorists ask when they first venture abroad. Fortunately, deciphering foreign signs is generally less of a problem than you might expect.

Most countries that British motorists are likely to visit have signed the 1968 Vienna convention on road signs and signals. That provided for a general harmonisation of signs, following the convention that:

▲ triangular signs **warn**

● circular signs **prohibit**

■ rectangular signs **inform**

ROAD **HAZARDS**

Under this convention the 'stop' sign is octagonal and the 'give way' sign is an upside down triangle. Because of their distinctive shapes, it's possible to recognise these signs even if they are obscured by snow or ice.

Conveniently for us, road signs across the world are often expressed in English even when that isn't the local mother tongue. English lends itself to short, sharp, catchy phrases, which apart from making life a lot easier for tabloid headline writers also makes it ideal for road signs. 'Give way' is a lot more pithy than '*cedez le passage*' in French, just as 'speed limit' is less of a mouthful than the German '*Geschwindigkeitsbeschrankung*'.

There is still a chance to get confused by foreign signs. Some common signs used abroad, such as the yellow diamond indicating that traffic on a road has right of way, are simply not used in Britain.

Sometimes a local phrase on a sign may need translating. In that case you may find it in the guide to individual countries at the back of this book, but it might also pay to equip your passenger with a pocket dictionary in case you encounter something out of the ordinary.

How signs are used can also catch out the unwary. The French are more sparing with bend signs than us. On a British motorway, a bend warning can herald a quite gentle curve; but if you see a bend sign on a French motorway expect to have apply the brakes and change down a gear to negotiate the corner.

Signs may also be smaller than you are used to, and mounted in a more obscure position on the road. When driving abroad you need to be constantly alert and actively looking for signs.

Traffic sign colours also vary between countries. Motorway directional signs in Britain, France, Germany and Spain are blue, but in Switzerland, Italy and Denmark they are green. In the UK and France, non-motorway trunk road directional signs are green, while in Italy they are blue.

Watch out for signs that look familiar but may not mean exactly what you expect. A sign warning of a right-hand bend in the road might indicate a more severe bend than you would expect if you encountered it in the UK

World of motoring
"In New Zealand almost every bend has an advisory speed limit, which is set at an accurate and dependable level. This aid to driving is so consistent that one must guard against getting caught out by the occasional unmarked bend."
Jonathan Sherwill

Handily enough for British motorists, the word 'stop' is an almost universal warning, although the configuration of junctions may still cause us a little confusion

World of motoring

"I nearly had a bad accident in Spain. At a left turn across oncoming traffic there are often road markings and signs to guide you off the road into a bay on the right, before crossing when the traffic is clear. But my trap was an unsigned example where the bay was just the verge. Not noticing, I tried to make the turn British style but overtaking cars assumed right of way and blared through three abreast."
Philip Reeve

Road markings

White lines on the road are an important source of information. Abroad as in the UK, the general rule is that the more paint there is on the road, the more serious the hazard to be negotiated. Often warnings are painted on a stretch of road only after there have been serious crashes there.

Other countries often put an unbroken white stop line where in Britain we might expect to see a more flexible 'give way' junction. These are usually clearly marked with the word 'stop', although you may see 'ârret' used in France and French-speaking Canada.

Stop always means stop, even if local drivers may not seem to acknowledge it. If you creep over a stop line without coming to a complete halt you're inviting the attention of the police. Take care in more remote areas where road maintenance is infrequent, as white lines can get so worn away that they become hard to spot, particularly under the glare of the summer sun.

An unbroken white line in the middle of the road means no overtaking, just as it does in Britain, but many countries including France use just a single line to prohibit overtaking in both directions.

How white lines are used to prohibit overtaking depends on the amount of forward visibility, but this varies from country to country. Never overtake unless you're completely sure there's sufficient space to do so safely, no matter what the road markings might say.

ROAD **HAZARDS**

Junctions

Road junctions can be confusing abroad, particularly during the first day or two when you are still getting used to driving on the right. Always be prepared for traffic coming from unexpected directions, and remember that where no other priority is marked, in most countries the rule is 'give way to the right'.

Spanish roads have a type of junction not found in Britain. When turning off a main road left into a side road across oncoming traffic, there is a turning circle provided on the right hand side of the road. Instead of stopping in the middle of the road and waiting for oncoming traffic to clear before turning, as you would in the UK, you are expected to pull off to the right of the road, then wait for traffic in both directions to clear before crossing the main road into the side road.

Similarly, when joining a main road you may have to drive all the way across the road to the turning circle and stop there before joining your carriageway.

At a crossroads, when you want to turn across oncoming traffic, and an approaching vehicle also wants to turn across your lane, the British *Highway Code* gives drivers two alternatives. The two cars can either pass in front, or drive around the back of each other. The second option is usually recommended because it means your view of oncoming traffic is not obscured by the other car. In other countries accepted practice may vary so make eye contact with the other driver to establish what he or she intends to do. In Italy, by law drivers must pass in front of each other in this situation.

In the US, at crossroads not controlled by traffic lights, priority is given to the vehicle which arrives at the stop line first. If two or more vehicles arrive at the same time than the rule is to give way to the right.

World of motoring

"New Zealanders have an unusual rule at junctions. If you are turning left into a minor road, you must give way to approaching traffic which is indicating to turn right into the same road. Be careful not to leave an indicator on after negotiating a junction, as you may end up with somebody turning across your path."
Andrew Jones

In Italy, if you intend to turn across another vehicle you must pass in front of it, not behind

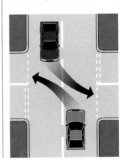

Extra care is needed on roundabouts, as in some countries vehicles entering the roundabout may have priority over those which are already on it.

Roundabouts

British drivers used to get in lots of trouble negotiating Continental roundabouts. The problem was that here at home, traffic entering the roundabout must give way to traffic already on the roundabout. In France and several other European countries, the opposite rule always used to apply: traffic on the roundabout had to stop and give way to traffic entering it.

Thankfully the rule on most Continental roundabouts has now been switched to the British system. In France this is indicated by a sign on the approach to the roundabout which says *Vous n'avez pas la priorité* (you do not have right of way) or *Cédez le passage* (give way). But beware that there are still a few roundabouts, mainly in rural areas, where the old rule still applies. So give way to traffic entering the roundabout if there is no sign expressly saying otherwise, and look out for the occasional local who isn't going to change the way they drive whatever the bureaucrats say.

In the US, roundabouts (*traffic circles* or *rotaries*) are very rare but you may come across them in some states. Before proceeding confidently across one of these, bear in mind that some American drivers may themselves never have encountered a roundabout before so expect the occasional confused reaction.

There are roundabouts (called 'rotaries') in America too, but they are few and far between

ROAD **HAZARDS**

Traffic lights

Traffic lights serve much the same function wherever you drive – stopping one stream of traffic to let another proceed – but there are some variations you need to watch out for.

Firstly you need to be much more observant to make sure you don't overlook traffic lights. In the UK we're used to lights being situated at a certain position and height beside the road. It's easy to miss traffic lights completely when they are smaller, a different shape and hanging from a wire slung across the road.

When you come to a halt at the stop line you may find that overhead traffic lights can no longer be seen no matter how far you crane your head. To get round this problem, there's usually a set of smaller lights set into the post at head height.

In most countries the traffic light sequence does not pass from red to red-and-amber before turning green. Instead the light switches straight from red to green without warning. This leaves you sitting with the car in neutral at a green light, with a sneaking feeling that you haven't been paying proper attention. In Austria you do get some warning, as the green light flashes before changing to red, and amber flashes on the way back from red to green.

In many countries you're likely to encounter a continuously flashing amber light. This means you can proceed if the road is clear, but you must give way to other vehicles or pedestrians. Sometimes you will have a green filter light, but still have to give way to pedestrians who also have the signal to cross.

One feature we don't have in the UK is a free turn on red. This means that traffic (driving on the right) can pass a red light to turn right, after first stopping to check the road is clear. First introduced in California in 1947, this rule has since been adopted by all American states but New York, as well as in Canada (except Quebec). It doesn't apply at all traffic lights, but where you aren't allowed to

43

World of motoring

"In Milan, traffic lights are instructions. In Rome, they are suggestions. In Naples, they are Christmas decorations."
Antonio Martino, Italian Defence Minister

The sequence and meaning of traffic light signals abroad can differ from those used in the UK

ROAD **HAZARDS**

In Australia, a stop sign with three black dots on it means that if the traffic lights are out of order or flashing amber, you must stop and give way to traffic as if at a junction controlled by a stop sign

World of motoring
"In Ecuador it's a common practice at traffic lights to overshoot the white line by such an extent that the overhead lights are no longer visible. When they turn green, the first driver in the queue is alerted that it's time to move by a fanfare of horns."
David Brigden

make this manoeuvre there should be a sign prohibiting it. Left turns (across oncoming traffic) are never permitted on red.

For British drivers who are used to red meaning stop under all circumstances, a free turn on red can take some getting used to, but it certainly speeds traffic flow. There is periodically talk of introducing it in the UK, and some European countries have already done so. In Germany, for instance, a sign with a green arrow at the traffic lights indicates it's okay to turn right on red.

In some countries the traffic light sequence may alter at night. A flashing red or amber signal is used, particularly in the US. Flashing red means you must stop and check the junction is clear before proceeding; flashing amber means slow down and exercise extra caution through the junction. In Germany it's common for the lights to be turned off completely overnight. In this case look for a give way or stop sign which tells you how to treat the junction when the lights are out.

On the whole British drivers obey traffic light commands and it's rare to see a really blatant example of jumping the red light. This isn't necessarily the case in other countries. In one year, 89,000 crashes and nearly 1,000 deaths were caused by drivers running red lights in the US.

Caution is needed to avoid becoming one of these statistics. Never drive off when the lights turn green without looking right and left to check that oncoming traffic really did stop when their lights changed to red.

And bear in mind that the driver following you may not expect you to slam on your brakes if you see a traffic light turn red, when in the same situation most locals would opt to hit the accelerator instead. To avoid the possibility of a rear-end shunt, slow down when approaching a green traffic light so if it does change you have time to stop gradually, allowing your brake lights to give plenty of warning to following drivers.

In many countries drivers do not stop to give way to pedestrians waiting at a zebra crossing. If you do decide to stop, check your mirrors first or you risk being rear-ended by a surprised local motorist

Pedestrian crossings

In Britain we have the habit of stopping at zebra crossings to let pedestrians walk across. Try this in many other countries and you're likely to take a following driver completely by surprise, resulting in a screech of brakes and if you're unlucky, a car ploughing into the back of yours. Do show courtesy to pedestrians but for safety's sake always check your rear view mirror before braking.

In many countries pedestrians are expected to cross only at designated crossings and can be charged with jay walking if they disobey. It's also commonly an offence to walk across a pelican crossing (one controlled by traffic lights) when the pedestrian crossing light shows red.

Railway crossings

On some rural roads a level crossing over a railway line may not be protected by gates which close when a train is approaching. There may be warning lights which flash to warn when a train is coming, but sometimes on quiet lines even these are lacking. This sort of crossing is quite common in back country America, and is potentially very dangerous. Do not drive across unless you are certain nothing is coming. Stop, wind down your window and listen for the sound of an approaching train, and if you're still not sure send out a passenger to check and wave you safely across.

World of motoring

"French drivers do not stop at zebra crossings and although it seems silly, a pedestrian waits until the traffic has gone before crossing. If you stop you'll probably have a bemused pedestrian staying rooted to the spot wondering why you have stopped. The risk then is that other traffic may start to overtake you, making it more dangerous if the pedestrian does decide to move."
Ron Harrington

Toll roads are common across the world and can add significantly to the cost of a long journey. Credit cards are usually accepted but it pays to keep some loose change handy just in case

World of motoring

"I have always used a Visa card to pay autoroute tolls in France, but in the last three years voucher tracing has become difficult. The Autoroute companies now consolidate each daily bill as one charge, sometimes combining several companies in one entry. In addition to keeping all bills in an envelope, my wife writes the last three digits of the car mileage on each voucher. This helps sort out the statements when you are back home."
Mike Jobling

Toll roads

Drivers must pay tolls to use motorways in many countries and British drivers may be unfamiliar with how the routine operates.

It's usually straightforward. As you join the motorway you are stopped by a barrier and have to take a ticket before it rises to let you pass. If you're travelling alone, this is when you'll miss having a passenger, as you'll need to stretch over to collect the ticket through the passenger window. Pulling up as tightly as possible to the ticket machine helps, but watch out for the high concrete kerbs which can do a lot of damage to alloy wheels and tyres.

Take care of your toll ticket; it's easy to mislay it in a car packed with books, maps and toys, and you don't want to be scrambling around searching for it while you hold up the queue at the other end. If you do happen to mislay the ticket, it means you'll be charged the maximum fee for that stretch of road.

When you leave the motorway, or the toll section ends, there is another set of booths and barriers; hand over your ticket to the attendant and the price you need to pay is indicated on a screen. Be careful not to get into the lanes (usually on the far left and signed *télépéage* in France) that are reserved for local cars with a season ticket.

On some roads, there is no first stage of picking up a ticket. You simply arrive at a set of payment booths where you pay a fixed sum. If you have the correct change, you may be able to save time by exiting through automatic barriers – you toss the coins into the bin provided and the barriers raise automatically.

Credit cards are acceptable in most countries, but it's always handy to keep some loose change in the car just in case.

ROAD **HAZARDS**

Tunnels

Today's major highways are built straight and level for speed, which poses a problem in hilly areas. Where roads originally snaked up and down between valley and mountain pass, road engineers now take a more direct approach, using tunnels and bridges to flatten out the landscape.

The big Alpine tunnels are breathtaking pieces of engineering: the St Gothard in Switzerland is the world's longest, 16km in length and over 1,000m above sea level. On a smaller but no less impressive scale, some motorways, such as those following Italy's rugged coastlines, traverse a continual succession of bridges and tunnels.

Because we have few road tunnels in the UK on anything approaching this sort of scale, they're a

Always put on your dipped headlamps when passing through a road tunnel. You must do this by law in most countries, whether or not the tunnel is lit

hazard that needs to be treated with particular caution when driving abroad.

The issue of tunnel safety has been highlighted by serious incidents in both Mt Blanc and St Gothard tunnels, in which fire claimed a total of 50 lives. In the event of a fire breaking out in a tunnel head straight for the emergency exits which will be clearly marked.

Crashes in tunnels can have particularly serious consequences because there is little space in which to take avoiding action. Always create extra space around your vehicle in a tunnel and keep well back from the vehicle in front. Reduce your speed and adhere strictly to the lower speed limits which are usually in force in the longer tunnels (the Mt Blanc tunnel now has strictly enforced limits for both speed and separation distance).

It can be disconcerting to plunge from bright Mediterranean sunshine into the black depths of a tunnel, then emerge blinking into the dazzling light again. Slow down as your eyes will need time to adjust to the changes (particularly if you are wearing sunglasses), and watch out for poorly lit slow-moving vehicles ahead of you.

Always put on your dipped headlamps in a tunnel even when it is well lit. This is compulsory in most countries, and there is usually a sign to remind you to switch your lamps on when approaching and off when emerging.

In winter you may need snow chains on the approach to a tunnel but they are not allowed inside. Lay-bys are provided for drivers to stop and remove their snow chains.

There is often a toll to pay at the major tunnels. In the Alps there are also a handful of rail tunnels, where you drive your car onto a train in a similar fashion to using Le Shuttle. These can be useful when severe weather closes road routes across the mountains. Check locally for departure times and advance booking if necessary.

Many tunnels and motorways abroad have minimum as well as maximum speed limits. The minimum permitted speed is indicated by a number in a blue circle

ROAD **HAZARDS**

Always treat cyclists with courtesy and leave them plenty of room when overtaking. Take special care where cycle lanes cross the road, as in some areas cyclists have right of way

Cyclists

Cycling is not nearly as popular in Britain as in other European countries such as France and the Netherlands.

Perhaps because they don't cycle personally, some British drivers display a cavalier attitude to cyclists. Cutting too close when overtaking a cyclist is a bad habit that's far too common here. In many European countries cyclists get more consideration. In the home of the *Tour de France*, the law states that motorists must leave a two-metre gap when overtaking a cyclist.

Cycle lanes are a particular feature of many European towns, and cyclists can have priority where British drivers may not expect it. Look out for signs indicting that cyclists have right of way when a cycle path crosses a road.

For years scooters have been a vivid expression of carefree Mediterranean life. Their use is becoming increasingly regulated by law, but they are still a special hazard in many cities of southern Europe

World of motoring

"Driving after dark in Romania brings fast, clear roads away from the main cities. But they have a unique motoring hazard. The local population still relies on horse, mule, donkey and cart for their transport. These regularly travel on main roads without lights. If you are very lucky, the driver may shine a small hand torch at you – by which time you will be braking very hard."
R H Corbett

Scooters

There was a time when every Mediterranean city buzzed with swarms of scooters. They were the preferred mode of travel for teenagers, being stylish, cheap to run and quicker than a car in crowded streets. Despite this advantage, scooter use has been declining in recent years, and scooterists in Italy have received a further blow to their cherished freedom now that the wearing of crash helmets is compulsory there.

But there are still plenty of scooters thronging the cities of Southern Europe, often ridden with abandon, showing a cavalier disregard for stop signs, traffic lights and one-way streets, overtaking left and right, and ultimately taking to the pavement when the road is blocked.

Keep in mind the old road safety slogan 'Think once, think twice, think bike' and be very cautious when turning right in town – there's probably a scooter creeping up in your blind spot.

ROAD **HAZARDS**

Trams

Trams are a common sight in many foreign cities. Regulations regarding trams vary from country to country. Generally they have priority over other traffic, especially when pulling away from a stop. Show extreme caution when overtaking. Passing a tram is generally permitted only on the right (between the tram and the pavement) but you must always give way to passengers getting on and off.

School buses

Some countries have strict laws prohibiting drivers from overtaking school buses when they stop to let down or pick up passengers.

In the US, for instance, you must come to a complete halt for a school bus that is stopped with red lights flashing. This applies whether you are following the bus or approaching it in the opposite lane. You must stop even if you are on a multi-lane highway. The only exception to this is a highway which is divided by a central reservation, in which case traffic in the opposite lanes does not have to stop but must slow down and pass with caution. American drivers obey this rule strictly, and overtaking a stationary school bus is treated seriously by the law.

Trams are a picturesque feature of cities such as Amsterdam (above); drivers should take care not to obstruct them and give way where required

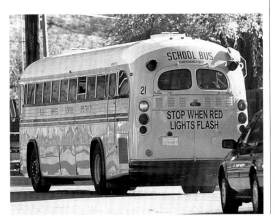

Do not drive past a stationary school bus with its red lights flashing, even if you are on the other side of the road

52

Domestic animals – such as these sheep in New Zealand – can be just as much a hazard on the road as their wild cousins

World of motoring

"Driving through Finland we saw numerous signs warning of the danger of reindeer on the road. These are no exaggeration. Reindeer blend with road surfaces, ditches and birch trees to the point of invisibility. They trot suicidally in front of the car, antlers laid back and eyes rolling. You slow down, they slow down. Steer to the left and they run to the left, steer to the right and they run to the right. Stop – and guess what! And they don't react to horn or lights."
Fiona Haig

Animals

Running over a rabbit or hedgehog can be distressing, but British wildlife rarely represents a physical danger to motorists.

It's a different story overseas. Hitting a large animal at speed can be enough to write off a car and kill or seriously injure its occupants.

Elk are a particular hazard in Scandinavian countries. These large deer stand six feet high at the shoulder, weigh up to half a tonne and have no road sense whatsoever. In some districts of Sweden they account for more than half of road traffic accidents. In a collision the front bumper hits the elk's legs, pivoting its body on to the bonnet and through the windscreen with potentially fatal results.

Elk are also found in Canada where they are called moose and represent a similar hazard. Keep your speed down when driving through wooded areas where they may run on to the road without warning. If you do hit a moose, you must report the accident to the police.

In Australia kangaroos are the problem – which is why drivers routinely fit 'roo-bars' to the front of their cars. The danger of hitting a kangaroo is greatest at night, so it makes a lot of sense to confine your driving in the outback to the daylight hours – especially as hire cars rarely come fitted with roo bars.

An instinctive reaction for many animals on encountering danger is to freeze, and this is precisely what they may do when they see a car bearing down towards them. This gives a chance to slow and steer round the animal. But in this situation do remember that your priority is the safety of yourself and other road users. Check for other traffic before swerving or slamming on your brakes.

Don't overlook the potential hazard of domestic animals on the road either. Always keep your speed down when driving through unfenced stock-rearing country, and remember that if a sheep or goat runs across the road in front of you, another is sure to

ROAD **HAZARDS**

follow. Don't speed up again until you're absolutely certain the coast is clear.

In farming areas you may pass through gates designed to keep stock in or out. Always leave a gate as you found it, open if it was open, closed if it was closed. Gates are usually left open for a reason – perhaps to let stock get to a water supply – so closing an open gate can have disastrous results. If travelling in convoy, the leading vehicle should wait by a gate until all the vehicles are through, to ensure the gate is left as it was found.

It's not only when your car is moving that you need to watch out for wildlife. Black bears in Yosemite National Park, California, have become expert at breaking into cars in search of food. In one year, 1,100 break-ins occurred, causing $400,000 of damage. It's claimed the bears target specific makes, with Honda and Toyota top of the list.

World of motoring
Visitors to Bavaria face an usual motoring hazard – the Pine Marten. These weasel-like creatures have acquired a taste for brake fluid, gnawing through the brake lines of parked cars to get at it. Drivers are advised to check their brakes before driving off after leaving their car in a forest parking area

One of Saab's managing directors was killed when his car hit an elk. Ever since, the Swedish manufacturer has carried out simulated elk crash tests and reinforces its cars to withstand such an impact

Emergency vehicles
In some countries, such as the United States, drivers are required by law to stop and let an emergency vehicle pass. There are also laws prohibiting motorists from following closely behind emergency vehicles, and stopping nearby while they are attending an emergency. Be prepared to give way to military and state vehicles too. In Zimbabwe, drivers must stop when they see the presidential cavalcade and let it pass.

RULES AND REGULATIONS

As usually law-abiding citizens, the one time that most of us are likely to fall foul of the law is on the road. Few drivers go through their motoring career without picking up the occasional parking ticket or speeding fine.

In most cases this is because drivers deliberately choose to break regulations, whether by driving at 85mph on the motorway or parking on double yellow lines to pop into the newsagents.

No-one wants their holiday spoiled by a run-in with the law, so it goes without saying that you should be on your best driving behaviour overseas. But there's the added problem that however carefully you drive, you may be caught out if you are unfamiliar with foreign laws. Ignorance of the law is no defence – although if you're lucky it may earn you a more sympathetic hearing from a local traffic cop.

This chapter gives an overview of the motoring regulations you're likely to encounter overseas, but for specific advice on laws in individual locations you should also consult the country by country advice at the back of this book.

55

Ignorance of the law is no defence: wherever you drive you need to know what the local speed limits and driving regulations are to avoid an expensive encounter with the police

Not all speed traps are as visible as this one in America. Speed cameras and radar are now so widespread that exceeding the speed limit can quickly earn you a fine – or worse – with no warning whatsoever

World of motoring
"I read in a Calais newspaper about a British Ferrari owner who had been stopped for speeding well over the limit and found his licence suspended and car impounded on the spot. The Editor remarked that 'the red stallion is in the police corral'."
Mike Jobling

Speed limits

There might be increasing harmonisation of regulations within Europe, but you wouldn't guess it to look at the variety of speed limits prevailing over the Continent. Driving at the legal French motorway limit of 130km/h (80mph) could earn you a small fine in Belgium, where the limit is 120km/h (75mph), but it would be a serious offence in Norway which has a lowly 90km/h (55mph) limit. On the German *Autobahn* you'd be within your legal rights to drive at 180mph; try that anywhere else in Europe and they'll lock you up and throw away the key.

It's a similar situation in the US, where each state sets its own limits and what is permissible on the freeway in Colorado (limit: 75mph) is decidedly illegal in New Jersey (limit: 55mph).

In general, police everywhere are cracking down on speeding. Exceed the stated limit and you're likely to receive an unpleasant shock to your wallet. Speed detection methods vary, but as the use of radar and cameras becomes both more widespread and sophisticated, it's easy to be caught speeding without any prior warning.

Police in France and Italy have a simple method of catching drivers who break the limit on toll motorways. Your toll ticket carries the time it was issued, so a quick calculation at the other end reveals your average speed: if you've covered 150km in 60 minutes, you will get a ticket.

Don't be caught out by urban speed limits on the Continent. By British standards the start of the speed limit may not be clearly signposted. Where no speed

RULES & **REGULATIONS**

limit is shown, you should assume that the urban speed limit starts where you see a signpost giving the name of the town or village. At the other side of town, a sign showing the place name crossed out indicates that the urban limit is ending. Look out for the sign *rappel* in France, which is a reminder that a restriction is still in force.

Be aware that the speed limit may change in poor weather. When it's raining the motorway limit in France drops from 130km/h to 110km/h. New drivers in France must also stick to lower speeds for two years after obtaining their full driving licence.

Lower speed limits may also apply when you are towing. In Germany, there is a blanket speed limit of 80km/h outside built-up areas for cars towing a trailer or caravan.

Long straight highways in the US are a temptation to put your foot down, but be careful there isn't a police aeroplane circling overhead. These are commonly used to spot speeding vehicles, radioing ahead to the next town where a traffic cop will be waiting to pull over the errant motorist.

One place which enforces its speed limits with particular rigour is the state of Victoria in Australia. Police there use mobile speed cameras on a grand scale to apprehend drivers exceeding the limit by the smallest margin.

Do not be tempted to take a radar detector abroad in an effort to evade speed traps. In most countries they are illegal, and you risk being fined and having both your detector *and* your car confiscated. The same applies to satellite navigation systems that have points of interest (POI) function able to display speed camera sites. These are prohibited in several countries, including Ireland, Germany and Switzerland, where you must keep the POI switched off to avoid a fine.

Don't dawdle either: many countries have minimum as well as maximum speed limits, particularly on motorways. In France the motorway minimum is 80km/h (50mph) in good weather.

Traffic lights are used in Spain to slow speeding vehicles. Placed at the approach to a town or village, they incorporate sensors to detect traffic speeds. If a vehicle approaches at above the speed limit, the lights turn red, forcing the driver to come to an embarrassed halt

Being under the influence of either alcohol or illegal drugs when driving is an offence that police across the world take very seriously. Break the law and you could be looking at a jail sentence

Drink-driving

The amount of alcohol you are allowed to consume before driving varies between countries. Most have a lower limit than the UK's 80mg alcohol per 100ml of blood. In France the limit was lowered a few years ago to 50mg. In Sweden the limit is just 20mg and in Eastern European countries such as Hungary and Slovakia you are not allowed to drink *anything* before driving.

Most countries treat drink-driving very seriously and police everywhere are increasingly cracking down on drivers who exceed the limit. Penalties can be severe: a heavy fine is certain and imprisonment a possibility.

The rule when driving abroad is simple: don't drink and drive. Even small amounts of alcohol can impair your concentration with possibly tragic results. Remember too that European bottled beer can be a lot stronger than what we're used to at home.

In some parts of America it is illegal even to have an alcoholic drink in the passenger compartment of a car. So if you buy a bottle of wine, make sure you put it in the boot.

Remember too that a legal drinking age of 21 is not unusual in many American states, so you may be old enough to drive but not yet old enough to drink. In Texas a zero tolerance policy on minors and alcohol means that anyone under the age of 21 who is found to have drunk any alcohol at all before driving is charged with driving under the influence of alcohol.

World of motoring
Canadian motorists convicted of drink-driving can have their suspension reduced if they agree to have an alcohol ignition interlock fitted to their car. This automatically tests the driver's breath and won't allow the engine to start if they've been drinking

RULES & **REGULATIONS**

Parking

Europe's crowded cities weren't designed with cars in mind and parking can be a nightmare – particularly because rules vary not only from country to country, but from town to town. And even in the same town rules may change depending on what time of day, week or year it is.

On some French streets an arrangement of alternate parking operates. From the 1st to the 15th of each month parking is permitted on one side of the street, then it switches to the other side of the road from the 16th to the end of the month.

Elsewhere parking is not allowed during rush hours, or overnight when street cleaning is carried out. In Japan parking is so tight you can't even buy a car without producing evidence that you have a parking space for it.

Penalties for illegal parking are just as varied. You may receive a ticket, but you're just as likely to find your car clamped or towed away. I once parked late at night on a street in Brussels, headed off to my hotel and returned early the next morning to find an empty space where my car had been. It wasn't until I spotted a tiny peeling red sticker on a nearby door that I realised the car hadn't been stolen but had been towed away in the early hours. I then had to trek halfway across town and pay a hefty fine to get it released.

The best option in an unfamiliar town is to find an official car park. You'll have to pay, but at least you know you aren't going to run foul of some obscure parking law and you're also better protected against a casual thief breaking into your car in the night.

If you do park on the street check the regulations carefully and if you have any doubt, ask the locals if it is okay to park there. Coloured paintwork on the kerb normally means some sort of parking restriction is in force. Parking with two wheels on the pavement is permissible in many countries as long as you allow enough space for pedestrians to get by.

Avoid parking in the vicinity of a road junction, a

Not all parking restrictions are marked as clearly as this, and a mistake can easily result in your car being clamped or towed

World of motoring
"When visiting one of the vast shopping malls in the US, such as the Mall of America in Minneapolis, make sure you remember where you left your car – it is very embarrassing to lose it and have to ask security for help."
John Kent

Parking in southern Europe can seem a free-for-all at times. In congested cities often the best plan is to park on the outskirts and catch a bus to town

World of motoring

"Read 'no parking' signs carefully when in the US. Sometimes one may not park at certain times of the night as the streets are cleaned in the early hours of the morning. In cities such as Washington DC, parking is banned along the appropriate side of the street during the rush hour, depending on the direction of travel."
Gareth Zimmerman

pedestrian crossing, a railway crossing, a police or fire station, a fire hydrant, near tram tracks, or where a hill or curve restricts visibility for oncoming traffic.

In village centres check for signs indicating market days, or you may return the next morning to find your car stranded in a sea of market stalls (as well as some very irritated stall holders).

In southern Europe double parking can be common, so be careful you don't park where you may find your car blocked in on your return.

Many continental countries operate blue zones which allow parking for a set period of time. You have to display a parking disc on your windscreen set to show your time of arrival. Discs are usually widely available from local shops, service stations and police stations.

Parking meters are also widespread. Some high-tech French versions require you to enter your car's registration number which is recorded on the ticket to prevent half-expired tickets being used twice.

In many countries it's illegal to park facing oncoming traffic. The police are particularly hot on this in North America and Australia, and it can catch out British drivers who are used to parking on either side of the road. We're not supposed to park here facing oncoming traffic at night, but it's one of those rules that some people don't seem to know exists.

Again in America, it's often a legal requirement when parking on a slope to leave your front wheels turned in towards the kerb, so if the parking brake fails the car won't run away.

In general, though, parking is easier and often free of charge in the New World. American towns usually provide an abundance of large, conveniently angled parking lots along the side of every street.

RULES & **REGULATIONS**

Disabled drivers

The disabled driver's blue badge is recognised throughout the EU. Disabled drivers displaying this badge are entitled to similar parking concessions to those they have in the UK.

In France these concessions vary according to the region of the country. Parking places reserved for disabled people are usually marked with a wheelchair symbol. Parking on the streets of Paris is free of charge if displaying the blue badge, and there are fee discounts when parking in off-street car parks.

Mobile phones

A mobile phone can be invaluable in keeping you in touch with home while travelling abroad. Most mobile phones can be used overseas, but you may need to arrange a roaming service with your provider beforehand.

Never use your mobile phone while driving. Crashes caused by drivers who are distracted by talking on the phone are a growing problem. Most countries ban using a hand-held mobile phone while driving, and in Spain only fully hands-free sets (without an earpiece or headphones) are permitted.

Vehicle lighting

It's been a legal requirement for some years in Scandinavian countries for drivers to use dipped headlights during daylight hours as well as at night, and some other European countries are adopting this practice. It applies in Italy, Slovenia and Hungary outside built-up areas, and in Poland during the winter months. Some Canadian provinces have a similar ruling.

In many places it is illegal to drive on sidelights alone, and some Eastern European countries outlaw using main beam while in built-up areas.

Many motorcyclists adopt the sensible practice of keeping their dipped headlamp on at all times to increase their visibility. This is actually a legal requirement in some countries, including France.

World of motoring
"In France I encountered the road sign *Entrée Interdite Sauf Riverains*, which translated means 'No entry except for local residents'. The hotel where I was staying could be reached using this road. I discovered from hotel management that I was quite entitled to use the road as long as I was residing at the hotel, and the same would apply to anyone staying at a gîte or hotel accessible via such a road."
André Fontaine

Wearing a seatbelt is usually compulsory and always good sense. Many countries impose a minimum age below which children cannot use the front seat unless they are in a child restraint

Seat belts

If you are involved in a car crash, wearing a seat belt can make the difference between life or death. Front seat belts are estimated to save around 370 lives each year in the UK. Rear seat belts save a further 140 lives even though fewer than half of adult passengers choose to wear them here.

A car travelling at 35mph covers 51 feet per second. In a head on collision with a solid object it takes just 150 milliseconds to come to rest. If the occupants are wearing seatbelts they could hope to emerge with minor cuts and bruises. Unrestrained, they would hurtle out of their seats with possibly fatal results. In such a crash, unbelted back seat passengers are catapulted into those travelling in the front seats at around the same speed as the vehicle was travelling when it crashed.

Wearing a seat belt is compulsory in most countries. Even in countries where the law is widely flouted, you should always take the precaution of wearing your seat belt, and ensure that front and rear seat passengers are also securely belted in.

Children in cars

If you have children on board you must always ensure they are properly restrained, using an approved child seat or booster seat where necessary. Many countries prohibit children under a certain age or height (typically 12 years and 1.5 metres) from sitting in the front passenger seat if rear seats are also available.

Remember never to place a rear-facing child seat in the front passenger seat of a car equipped with an airbag unless there is a means of deactivating the airbag. The impact of the airbag exploding during a crash could prove fatal.

RULES & **REGULATIONS**

Loading your car

It's inevitable that any family heading off on holiday in their car is sure to pack it to the gills with luggage. Always check tyre pressures before driving a heavily laden car, and if necessary inflate them in accordance with the instructions in the manufacturer's handbook. Your car may be slower to respond when laden so take corners more cautiously and leave extra braking distance. Try to spread the weight evenly throughout the car. Heavy objects in the boot cause the front suspension to lift, making the steering feel light and reducing your control over the car.

Remember to adjust the headlamp beams when driving a fully laden car. Heavy loads, particularly in the boot, depress the rear of the car, causing the headlamp beams to be deflected upwards which can dazzle oncoming drivers. Most cars have a switch on the dashboard that allows you to compensate the headlamp angle for the load on board.

Always secure loads properly, and never stack boxes above head height: they could catapult forward with tragic consequences if you have a crash or perform an emergency stop.

A roof box can be a good idea if you need to carry lots of luggage. This generates less wind resistance than stashing belongings on a roof rack, cutting noise and saving fuel. It also can be locked for extra security. If you do use a roof rack, try to keep the load as low as possible, and avoid putting very heavy items on it as this will raise the car's centre of gravity and reduce its stability.

Drivers may be tempted to overload their cars when popping over to France to stock up on beer and wine. Police on both sides of the Channel are cracking down on drivers of dangerously overloaded vehicles – and the resulting fine will more than wipe out the financial benefits of buying cheap goods in France. For major shopping trips, leave your car at home and hire a van instead.

A lockable roof box is better than a roof rack when driving long distances – it's quieter, more fuel efficient and offers much better protection against theft

Don't forget to padlock bicycles securely in place when carrying them on a cycle rack, as they are a tempting target for thieves

Carrying bicycles

If carrying bicycles for long distances abroad ensure you have a sturdy rack and security system, and that your rear numberplate is not obscured.

Vehicles in Italy must display a reflective square warning panel on any overhanging load, including bicycles attached to the rear of a car.

Crossing the Channel

Getting your car across the Channel has been easier than ever since the Eurotunnel railway service joined traditional ferry crossings. Motorhomes and caravans are carried on Eurotunnel and most ferry services, although it pays to check and book in advance because spaces are limited and can fill up rapidly at peak periods.

Check with the operator if you intend carrying spare fuel in a can – this may not be permitted or only in small quantities. And don't fill your tank right to the brim just before boarding – fuel could leak from the tank overflow during a rough crossing. No gas-powered cars are permitted to use Eurotunnel.

Passengers are not permitted to remain on the ferry car deck during the crossing. On Eurotunnel, driver and passengers remain with their vehicles for the 35-minute journey under the Channel. You are free to get out of your vehicle and walk around, and toilet facilities are provided. Smoking is forbidden both on ferry car decks and in Eurotunnel.

Don't overlook the alternative of taking a longer ferry trip, for instance to Le Havre, Roscoff or even Santander in northern Spain. This cuts the number of miles you have to drive, and you can travel overnight on the ferry to make a fresh start on your arrival in the morning.

Motorail is another option worth considering if you want to avoid the long drive to the south of France. Cars join the Motorail service at Calais bound for a number of destinations including Nice, Avignon and Toulouse. Check if you have a larger vehicle as some people carriers and off-roaders cannot use the service, and LPG-powered cars are not permitted.

Customs and Excise

Cigarette and alcohol smuggling from the continent is a major headache for the authorities – an astounding one in five cigarettes smoked in the UK is said to be smuggled. Consequently, Customs and Excise keep a careful watch at entry ports, and the penalties for smuggling are serious – including confiscation of your vehicle. You are advised to stay within the limits recommended by Customs and Excise (*see right*).

Remember that whatever you bring back must be strictly for your personal consumption or as a gift. It is not permitted to purchase cigarettes or alcohol for friends or family who intend to reimburse you, even if they are paying you only the cost price.

Customs limits

3200	cigarettes
400	cigarillos
200	cigars
3kg	tobacco
10	litres of spirits
20	litres of fortified wine
90	litres of wine
110	litres of beer

Book ahead to be assured of a place on a ferry, especially at peak periods.

If police stop you and hand out a fine, in many countries they will expect to be paid on the spot – even if that means escorting you to the nearest cash point to get enough money

World of motoring

"In America the stop sign means 'stop', even in the middle of the desert with a clear view and no traffic in sight. Ignore this at your peril. The police pulled over my partner in a campsite at 10pm for not stopping fully (he slowed almost to standstill but this wasn't enough). I asked my sister who lives in LA how long one should come to a halt at a stop sign and it seems that to count to three is the accepted rule."
Alexandra Metcalf

Dealing with the police

If stopped by the police in the UK, you'd naturally pull over, get out of your car and reach into your jacket for your driving licence.

Do this in America and you'd probably find yourself looking down the barrel of a gun.

American law enforcement officers have to live with the fact that an awful lot of Americans routinely carry firearms. If they stop you, they are going to be extremely cautious until they've established that you're not about to wave a shotgun at them.

So if you do get pulled over, stop the car, wind down the driver's window, turn off the ignition and sit with your hands on top of the steering wheel where they can be clearly seen.

It's easy to panic and jam on the brakes when a police car lights up behind you, but you should try to find a safe place to stop within a reasonable distance and not come to a sudden halt on a bend or where you will obstruct other traffic. In America, a patrol car will shine a red light at you as the signal that you should pull over, and this may be accompanied by a powerful loudspeaker command. You may be told where to pull over, for instance by coming off a freeway slip road.

Foreign police have a tendency to look threatening to anyone accustomed to the British bobby. Our police are unusual in that they are not usually armed and nor do they tend to adopt *Judge Dredd* style shades and leather. In many countries the police do, however, expect a high degree of respect. Be polite and co-operative, and in the vast majority of cases you will find they respond helpfully, and will be

RULES & **REGULATIONS**

prepared to be lenient when they find a visiting motorist has made an honest mistake.

In some countries there are police whose job is specifically to deal with motorists. California, for instance, has the CHP (California Highway Patrol). Italy has no fewer than four police forces, of which both the *Vigili Urbani* (local police) and *Carabinieri* (national police) can stop and fine motorists.

Stories abound of countries, mainly in the Third World, where police are said to stop motorists on trumped up charges in order to extract bribes. As a visitor it can be all too easy to misread such a situation with potentially serious consequences. Never attempt to offer a bribe. If you do find yourself in a situation where you think you are being invited to offer a bribe, respond with an attitude of polite incomprehension and the official should lose patience and let you go on your way.

On-the-spot fines

Foreign police know only too well that when they hand out a fine for a traffic offence, a visiting motorist may be tempted to ignore it in the knowledge that he'll be safely across the border by the time the deadline for paying it expires. The police

World of motoring
Expect to see the French police cruising in some unusually fast and flashy patrol cars. The National Assembly has passed a proposal to allow traffic police to keep and use the vehicles they seize. Civil servants have denied that this might lead to police harassing drivers to get hold of their high-performance motors

Foreign police can look intimidating at first sight, but in most cases they turn out to be helpful and interested to talk to visitors to their country

World of motoring
In Finland a wealthy entrepreneur was fined an incredible £50,000 for breaking the speed limit. This wasn't a clerk's error: Finnish traffic fines reflect the size of the transgressor's income as well as the severity of the offence

get round this problem by issuing fines that must be paid there and then. Most European police are empowered to hand out an on-the-spot fine for less serious motoring offences such as speeding. In France this can be up to €375.

The on-the-spot fine may just be a deposit for a larger fine, in which case you can expect a bill to arrive at your home address in due course. At the moment there is no mechanism whereby a court in one country can enforce payment of a fine for a motoring offence once the driver who committed it has returned to their own country. Neither can a driver receive penalty points on their British driving licence for an offence committed abroad. However, this is likely to change if a proposed EU convention on the mutual recognition of penalties comes into force: the first step in this direction has already been taken – a driving disqualification handed out in Ireland will be enforced in the UK too, and vice versa.

In most countries credit cards are not accepted in payment for an on-the-spot fine and if you don't have the necessary cash on you the police will escort you to the nearest cash machine to obtain it. A Eurocheque is sometimes acceptable. Always ask for a receipt when paying an on-the-spot fine.

You could of course contest an on-the-spot fine, in which case you would have to pay a deposit, but given the delay and inconvenience this would involve, and the possibility of having to return to appear in court, it's best simply to pay up and go on your way.

More serious offences, such as drink-driving or dangerous driving, could result in the police confiscating your licence. In this case you will have to find someone else to drive your car back to Britain.

You should also be cautious if you already have a number of penalty points on your licence. If you commit an offence in another country that would attract penalty points there, the police may check your licence to see if the addition of these points would result in your disqualification. If so, your licence may be confiscated and you will have to find some other way to get yourself – and your vehicle – home.

RULES & **REGULATIONS**

Towing abroad

Towing a trailer abroad opens up a whole new range of travel possibilities, such as taking camping gear for the family or canoes for an adventure holiday.

Don't be over-optimistic about the amount you can tow. A small camping trailer which does not have its own braking system should not exceed 750kg or more than half the car's kerb weight, whichever is the lower figure. Larger braked trailers and caravans should not be heavier than 85 per cent of the car's kerb weight, or the manufacturer's recommended towing weight if this is lower.

Weight distribution is important too. The trailer should always be slightly nose heavy. Once the trailer is hitched up to the car, run your eye along them from the side: if properly loaded, there should be a slight V-shape towards the coupling. The centre of the towball should be 350 to 420mm from the ground.

The towing bracket itself must be a European type approved model for any car registered after August 1 1998.

Just as in the UK, a car towing a trailer is subject to lower speed limits in many European countries. See the information on individual countries at the back of this book for details. France is an exception to this

Towing is a specialised driving skill and it's good advice to get some practice on familiar roads before heading overseas. Remember that speed limits are often lower when you are towing

A poorly loaded caravan can become unstable, particularly in high winds or sudden manoeuvres. Never overload a caravan or try to tow a heavier outfit than your car is designed to cope with

rule, and in theory you are permitted to tow at 130km/h (80mph) on the autoroute. You'd be better advised to stick to something nearer the 60mph (100km/h) UK motorway limit for car and trailer, particularly if you have little experience of towing. A car can be more susceptible to crosswinds when towing, it is more easily unsettled by sudden high-speed manoeuvres and stopping distances will be increased.

You must ensure that the tyres on your trailer are designed for a speed of 130km/h when towing in France, or you could risk a fine even if driving at a lower speed.

If your trailer is fitted with rear lights check they are working each time you couple up the trailer. You must also attach a GB sticker to the back of a trailer or caravan (unless europlates are fitted – see p83).

If you intend to tow a boat, bear in mind that all except the smallest boats need to be registered when used abroad. The body to apply to is the Small Ships Registry. You can obtain an application form from most yacht clubs and marinas.

Because towing puts an extra strain on the car you should give it a thorough inspection before leaving. Check the health of the rear shock absorbers in particular. Their life expectancy can be shortened if you do a lot of towing, and it can be a good idea to replace them with heavy-duty shock absorbers.

Be particularly cautious when tackling alpine passes, keeping an eye on your car's engine temperature to make sure it doesn't start to overheat. Some alpine roads are closed to caravans so equip yourself with a map which indicates these restrictions.

Towing a caravan

Making sure your car is powerful and stable enough to tow your caravan is a vital first step when embarking on a touring holiday abroad. Consult your manufacturer if you are in any doubt.

RULES & **REGULATIONS**

The noseweight of the caravan has a pronounced effect on its stability, and can be affected by the distribution of luggage inside it. You should aim for a noseweight of 25 to 75kg.

Don't go anywhere without checking that the caravan is in good working order. Tyres may not wear much but can deteriorate with age. Check for signs of cracking on sidewalls or between treads. Any suspect tyre should be replaced, and it's a good idea to replace any tyre over five years old. Don't forget to take a spare wheel when taking your caravan abroad, especially as some caravan tyre sizes are hard to obtain overseas.

Check that your door mirrors give a good view down the side of the caravan. If not, invest in a set of extension mirrors. Remember to remove or fold these flat when driving solo or you could fall foul of the law.

Caravanners need to be particularly wary of crosswinds on bridges and exposed motorway sections. These can cause the outfit to sway and in extreme conditions to snake out of control. Trying to correct this by steering or hitting the brakes is likely to make the situation worse. Instead, ease off the accelerator gently to reduce speed. A stabiliser can be fitted to reduce the risk of snaking – but don't rely on a stabiliser to overcome problems caused by poor loading in the first place.

A family on a caravanning holiday carries a lot of luggage, and it's important to stow it correctly. As much as possible should be put in the caravan itself, not in the boot of the car, and heavy items should be stowed low down over the caravan's axle. People are not permitted to travel in a moving caravan here or abroad.

Make sure you are completely confident about reversing your caravan. This manoeuvre takes a lot of practice to perfect, so it's a good idea to take a training course and master it thoroughly before venturing abroad, rather than finding yourself in a panic trying to reverse your outfit down a narrow mountain road.

To reverse a caravan you have to turn the steering in the opposite direction to where you want to go – it's a technique that takes practice to master

DOCUMENTS AND ACCESSORIES

Travel between EU countries is now so easy that you can drive across Europe without ever being stopped at a customs post. But don't let this deceive you into thinking you can drive in Europe with no more than the documents and insurance you need in the UK. Before taking a car abroad it's vital to make sure your paperwork is in order, and that you take with you everything that local police might ask to see if they stop you.

This includes accessories such as a warning triangle, which is a legal requirement in most of Europe but not in the UK.

Essential items can easily be overlooked, especially when just popping over to France for a day trip, and drivers don't realise the potential hassle they are letting themselves in for until they are involved in an accident and the police arrive.

Don't venture abroad without taking your driving licence, insurance details, registration document and all other official paperwork that police may ask to see if they stop you

The latest photocard British driving licence is recognised throughout Europe. It makes a lot of sense to upgrade to one if you still have an old pink or green licence

Driving licence

The first essential is your full valid driving licence. Keep it with you at all times. In the UK, there is no legal requirement to carry your licence. If you don't have it when the police ask to see it, they allow you seven days' grace in which to present it at a nominated police station.

The situation is quite different in most other countries. The police expect to see your licence on the spot when they stop you and you are committing an offence if you can't produce it.

The UK driving licence has changed its format twice in recent years. Some drivers have the pink licence that was introduced in 1990 and a few still have the green licence that preceded this, but most now have the current photocard licence that the DVLA started to issue in 1998.

Broadly speaking, the more recent the type of licence you have, the more convenient it is for foreign travel. The photocard licence conforms to European Union standards so is acceptable in all member states. It has other benefits too. In many countries there's a legal requirement to carry photo identification at all times, which for British visitors usually means carrying your passport on your person. The UK photocard driving licence is acceptable as ID instead. You can keep it on you even when you're not driving, and leave your passport in the security of the hotel safe. If you have a green or pink licence, you'll have to keep your passport with you in case police want to see it to confirm your identity.

Police tend to be lenient when they come across tourists who aren't carrying identification, but in some countries, such as India, British visitors have experienced great inconvenience – including a trip to

Minimum driving age
Recently qualified drivers should be aware that although they can obtain a licence in the UK at 17, in most European countries the minimum driving age is 18. New drivers are also subject to lower speed limits in France and Portugal

the cells – when they haven't been able to produce ID on demand.

If you're planning to drive abroad regularly, it makes a lot of sense to upgrade to a photocard licence. To do this, get application form D750 from a post office. This must be signed by a professional person (doctor, teacher), and sent to the DVLA along with a passport photograph and your passport or birth certificate. There's a small fee for this but if you are also notifying the DVLA of a change of address you don't have to pay anything. Allow three weeks for the DVLA to process the application and return your new licence.

Although your UK licence allows you to drive in a foreign country for a period of time sufficient for a holiday or business trip, you should investigate local regulations if you intend to stay for more than a few months or take up permanent residence.

International Driving Permit

An International Driving Permit (IDP) is recognised around the world. It acts as proof that you have a valid home licence and is printed in ten languages including Arabic, Russian and Chinese.

Many countries require you to carry an IDP along with your normal driving licence (the IDP is not sufficient on its own). Inside the EU you do not strictly speaking need an IDP unless you are still using one of the older, green, driving licences, which local police may not recognise.

However, as more time passes police in all EU countries are less likely to be familiar with either the older pink or green British licences, so to avoid any possible confusion it is a good idea to back up your licence with an IDP, or better still switch to a photocard licence.

You can obtain an IDP from one of the motoring organisations (such as the AA, RAC or Green Flag) whether or not you are a member. You need to send your current driving licence and a passport photograph along with the application form and fee (currently £7.50).

You must keep your licence and documents with you at all times when driving abroad and be ready to produce them on the spot if the police demand to see them

World of motoring
Don't forget your passport. You may have no trouble getting into France or Belgium, but getting back into the UK may not be so easy. Make sure it's in good condition if you're heading further afield. Border officials in some Eastern European countries can be reluctant to accept a tatty passport

Registration document
You must always carry your vehicle's registration document (V5) when you take your vehicle abroad. If you are stopped the police will want to see this to confirm that you are the owner of the vehicle.

If you have only recently purchased your vehicle, you may not yet have received its registration document. In this case you should apply to your local Vehicle Registration Office for a Temporary Certificate of Registration (V379). To do this, pick up a form V62 from the post office, and send it along with the bill of sale and proof of identity, plus the fee (currently £3).

If your vehicle is a company car, you need to ask your fleet manager to supply you with its registration document before you leave. You also need a letter on company notepaper stating that the driver is authorised by the registered owner to use the vehicle. If driving to Portugal, this isn't sufficient and you need a special certificate which motoring organisations can supply.

If the vehicle is leased, not owned, the leasing company will need to supply a vehicle on hire certificate (form VE103). This document confirms that you have the permission of the leasing company to take the vehicle out of the UK. You'll also need one of these certificates if you have hired a rental car that you plan to take abroad.

Give your fleet manager plenty of notice if you intend taking your company car abroad. Some companies don't like to hand over the actual V5 registration document. If you have to accept a photocopy of the registration document instead, make sure it is certified with the company stamp and an official signature.

DOCUMENTS AND ACCESSORIES

MOT certificate

If your vehicle is more than three years old you should take its current MOT certificate. Police may ask to see this in the event of an accident.

Vehicle Excise Duty

Car tax is usually renewable up to a maximum of two weeks in advance. This can be a problem if you are going to be out of the country for a longer period and your tax is due to expire while you are overseas. In these circumstances the DVLA allows a vehicle to be relicensed up to six weeks in advance, either by post to a head post office or by post or in person at a DVLA local office. You will need to provide a letter explaining why you need to apply so far in advance. If you give an overseas address, the tax disc can be sent to you there.

Motor insurance

The last thing you want to worry about when driving abroad is whether you are adequately covered by insurance in the event of an accident or theft from your vehicle. Don't embark on a trip abroad – even if it's just a day trip across the Channel – without first confirming with your insurer that you have adequate cover.

By law all UK motor insurance policies automatically provide third party cover in all EU member states (listed right). The same level of cover should also apply to the following non-EU countries (but you should check your policy beforehand to make sure): Czech Republic, Gibraltar, Hungary, Iceland, Liechtenstein, Monaco, Norway, San Marino, Slovakia, Slovenia, Switzerland.

Third party insurance cover means that if you are involved in an accident your insurer will cover the costs of vehicle repair or personal injury sustained by someone else. Your insurer will *not* pay for repairs to your own vehicle or any personal medical care and will not give any compensation or cover the costs of hiring alternative transport if your vehicle is unusable after an accident. Third party cover means

EU members
Austria
Belgium
Bulgaria
Cyprus
Czech Republic
Denmark
Estonia
Finland
France
Germany
Greece
Hungary
Ireland
Italy
Latvia
Lithuania
Luxembourg
Malta
Netherlands
Poland
Portugal
Romania
Slovenia
Slovakia
Spain
Sweden
UK

Accidents can happen, and if you are involved in a crash abroad you will be very relieved that you took out adequate insurance beforehand

World of motoring
US-style litigation is showing signs of coming to Europe. When a British businessman driving in France fell asleep and swerved off the road he forced the following vehicle to veer off the road too. The other driver was physically uninjured, but claimed more than £80,000 in damages for shock and stress

you are not covered if your vehicle is stolen or for the cost of any items lost if it is broken into.

This level of cover is clearly inadequate when driving abroad and you are highly recommended to upgrade to fully comprehensive cover. Give your insurer the dates of your intended trip well in advance of leaving and it will extend the same level of insurance cover you have in the UK to while you are abroad. Some insurers do this free of charge, while others (particularly direct insurers who offer cut-price premiums) may ask for an extra payment. If you plan to take your car abroad frequently then it's well worth checking these costs and taking them into account when you renew your insurance.

Also consider increasing your legal expense cover, as making claims for compensation in other countries can be difficult, expensive and time-consuming.

Make sure your insurer sends you a European Accident Statement. You will need to use this to record the details if you are involved in a crash while driving abroad.

Your insurance policy should cover any damage caused to your car while on a recognised ferry route, but if you are planning a voyage of longer than 65 hours, or an unusual route, consult your insurance company first.

Personal insurance

If you are involved in an accident abroad medical treatment can be extremely expensive. Always arrange personal travel insurance in addition to your motor insurance, or any insurance you take out on a hire car (although do check you're not simply paying twice over for the same level of cover).

The Foreign Office recommends that travellers take out a minimum of $500,000 of cover for hospital treatment and medical evacuation to the UK when heading to the United States.

EU member states operate a reciprocal healthcare scheme. You can get access to emergency medical care free of charge if you have a European Health Insurance Card (EHIC). This is a useful back up to have if you are just taking a day trip to France, but for any longer trips abroad comprehensive travel insurance is recommended. Some insurers may waive the medical excess on their policies if you have an EHIC.

Green Card

Many motorists believe they need to have a Green Card to be insured overseas. In fact, a Green Card provides no insurance cover in itself – it is simply an internationally recognised document that confirms that the holder has the minimum insurance cover required in the country being visited.

It is no longer obligatory to have a Green Card when travelling within the EU, or to any of those non-EU states where your UK insurance policy automatically gives you third party protection. It can still be a good idea to take a Green Card when driving to these countries, however, as it serves as instantly recognisable proof of third party insurance if at any time you are asked to demonstrate this. If you don't have a Green Card, you should always carry your certificate of insurance.

Countries that require a Green Card are listed on the right. The list is subject to change, so if in doubt check the information provided on the Association of

Countries that require a Green Card
Albania
Belarus
Bosnia-Herzegovina
Iran
Israel
Macedonia
Moldova
Morocco
Serbia & Montenegro
Tunisia
Turkey
Ukraine

Breaking down abroad can be an expensive and time-consuming process unless you have taken out comprehensive breakdown cover before leaving

British Insurers' website: www.abi.org.uk. If you do not have a Green Card when you arrive at one of these countries you may have to pay for insurance cover at the border.

Insurance companies do not charge for a Green Card, but if you have arranged your insurance through a broker it may levy an administration fee for arranging one.

Breakdown cover

No matter how comprehensive your insurance, it won't help if your car breaks down half a continent away – which is why you shouldn't venture abroad without some form of breakdown cover.

According to motoring organisations, 1 in 23 UK motorists need assistance while on holiday abroad, and it can cost over £2,000 to have a stranded car and four passengers brought home from southern Europe.

There's the convenience factor to consider too. You don't want to spend precious days of your holiday waiting for your car to be repaired in a backwoods garage. As well as roadside assistance and vehicle recovery, your policy should cover the cost of hiring a car so you can continue your holiday uninterrupted. The better schemes include useful extras such as spare parts location (helpful when your car is not a popular make locally), accommodation expenses, a message service, legal expenses and a replacement driver in the event that the only qualified driver is declared unfit to drive after an accident.

Vignettes

Some countries (Austria, Switzerland, Czech Republic, Slovakia) don't have motorway tolls but operate an alternative system of taxing motorists. You have to buy a tax disc, known as a vignette, which must be displayed on the windscreen before you can use the motorway system. Vignettes can be purchased at border crossings, or are available at petrol stations and post offices. If you are towing you may need to purchase two vignettes, one for the car and one for the trailer/caravan.

In Austria vignettes are available for periods of ten days, two months or one year. The vignette allows you 15 per cent discount on some tunnel toll fees.

In Switzerland the only vignette available is valid for one year (it actually runs from December to January 14 months hence).

Don't try to avoid purchasing a vignette or you risk being stopped by the police and fined.

Driving glasses

If you need to wear spectacles while driving, you should always carry a spare pair with you. This is commonsense wherever you are, but in Spain and Switzerland it's a legal requirement and you risk a fine if you aren't carrying a spare pair of glasses or prescription sunglasses.

If you need to wear glasses when driving, you should take a spare pair with you when going abroad. This is required by law in some countries

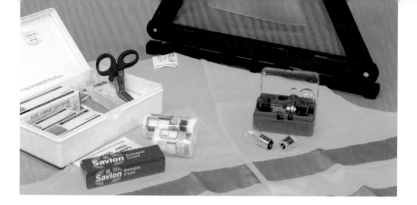

Different countries each have their own rules laying down what items of equipment must be carried in a car. Buy or put together yourself a kit that will meet the law in the countries you are driving through

Essential accessories

Every country in Europe specifies that certain accessories must be carried in the car. Well actually one country doesn't – the UK – which means many drivers head overseas lacking items of equipment that could earn them a fine if stopped by the police. The accessories you may need are:

◆ **Warning triangle**
   You must place a triangle on the road behind your car to warn other drivers should you break down or have an accident. Strictly speaking, in France you are permitted to use hazard warning lights instead of a triangle, but if your hazards are damaged in an accident then you are breaking the law if you don't display a triangle. In both Spain and Turkey you must carry two triangles.

◆ **Spare light bulbs**
   In France and many other countries it is illegal to drive with a defective light. If the police stop you because of this you must be able to replace the bulb on the spot or face a fine. Hence it is essential to carry a set of spare bulbs.

◆ **Reflective jacket**
   Many countries (including Austria, Belgium, Croatia, France, Italy and Spain) require the driver to carry a reflective jacket and wear it if they need to get out of the car at the roadside following an accident or breakdown. In some countries any passenger who exits the car also needs to wear one, so it's best to carry a reflective jacket for every person who is travelling in your vehicle.

◆ **First aid kit**
   Compulsory in Austria, Greece and several Eastern European countries. A standard first aid kit contains a variety of bandages, dressings, and antiseptic cream. Kits are available from chemists.

◆ **Fire extinguisher**
   Small fire extinguishers are available at most motor accessory shops.

All these are sensible items to have on board whether you are driving abroad or in the UK, so the best approach is to buy them and keep them permanently in your car. Kits containing these items and aimed specifically at motorists heading for Europe are available from motoring organisations, car manufacturers and motor accessory shops.

GB sticker

A national identifier or GB sticker is required by law when driving a UK-registered vehicle abroad. Place it as near to the rear numberplate as possible, and don't forget you also need one for your trailer or caravan if you are towing. If your car is fitted with the europlate (a numberplate that includes the EU symbol with the letters GB beneath it) you do not need a GB sticker while travelling within the EU.

Headlamp beam adjustment

Headlamps are designed to project a precise pattern of light. On a right-hand-drive car the dipped beam is higher on the left, to give better vision along the side of the road, and lower on the right, to avoid dazzling oncoming drivers.

Take your car abroad and the pattern is reversed, with the left beam now angled straight into the eyes of oncoming drivers. To avoid this, you need to fit headlamp beam converters. These blank out the part of the beam that might dazzle oncoming drivers abroad. It is compulsory to fit these to avoid running foul of the law overseas, but you must remember to remove them on your return to the UK.

If your car is fitted with the latest high-intensity discharge or xenon headlamps then masks will not work. Check your manual as you should be able to switch the beam to a left-hand-drive setting – but it may be necessary to consult your dealer.

Some cars, such as certain Citroëns, have headlamps that can be replaced very easily, so if you travel abroad often it may be worth purchasing a spare set of left-hand-drive lamps and swapping them over whenever you leave the country.

83

Vehicles driven abroad must show a national identifier. For cars from Great Britain and Northern Ireland the identifier is GB (above); Alderney (GBA), Guernsey (GBG), Jersey (GBJ) and the Isle of Man (GBM) have their own individual codes

If your car is fitted with europlates which show the GB symbol, a separate GB sticker is not required when visiting EU countries

Fuel can

A spare fuel can might seem a sensible accessory to take abroad but in fact it's best avoided. In some countries, such as Greece, carrying spare fuel in a car is illegal. Ferry companies may also not permit fuel cans on board, and Eurotunnel has restrictions on the type and number of cans.

The only time a fuel can is recommended is if you are heading through a desert or to a very remote area. In mainland Europe you are unlikely to have any problems obtaining fuel. For peace of mind, never wait until the empty light is blinking before stopping for fuel, fill up before you head off the beaten track, and don't rely on finding fuel on Sundays or national holidays.

Camping Card International

Indispensable for anyone heading on a camping or caravanning holiday abroad, the Camping Card International (CCI) is an ID card accepted at campsites across the Continent. It brings a number of other benefits, including discounts at many sites and tourist attractions, as well as third party liability insurance cover. In both Denmark and Portugal anyone wishing to stay at a camp site must have a CCI. Norway and Sweden have their own compulsory card. The CCI is available from motoring organisations or to members of camping and caravanning clubs.

If heading abroad for a camping holiday, don't forget to take a Camping Card International. It brings a number of discounts and benefits, and is compulsory when camping in some countries

Pet Travel Scheme

Dog and cat owners can take advantage of the Pet
Travel Scheme which allows them to take their pet
in and out of the country without the need for a
lengthy stay in quarantine. The scheme is restricted
to certain countries, including most of Europe, and
operates only at certain routes back into Britain.
There's a lot of red tape to go through too: the
animal must be vaccinated against rabies,
microchipped for identification, deloused and
wormed both sides of the Channel and
accompanied by health certificates. There is also the
option of an EU 'pet passport'. There are no restrictions
on taking pets between the UK and the Republic of
Ireland.

 If taking a pet abroad, bear in mind that some
countries have stricter rules concerning dogs in cars
than the UK. You must take steps to ensure that the
dog is not able to distract the driver; in Spain the dog
must be restrained or isolated from the driver and in
Italy if two or more dogs are carried they must be
kept caged or behind bars in the back of the car.

*Britain's once strict
quarantine laws have been
relaxed to allow pet
owners to take their
animals abroad – but the
procedure is complicated*

HIRING
A CAR

Today's independent travellers are more likely than ever before to hire a car when they get to their holiday destination. When visiting a popular holiday area, a hire car gives you the chance to get out of your bustling resort and explore the local countryside – which can be surprisingly unspoilt. You can search out secluded beaches, and discover sites of interest which are often free of crowds because they aren't on the itinerary of the major tour operators.

There are pitfalls to be navigated, both in ensuring you get the best hire deal and making sure you don't run into trouble by failing to read the small print of the rental contract. Drivers hiring abroad for the first time also face the new experience of handling a left-hand-drive car.

87

Cars are easy to hire in most popular holiday destinations, and provide an excellent way to get to know the local area

Cars in America tend to be bigger than in the UK, but roads and parking spaces are wider too, so driving a large car there is a lot easier than on narrow British streets. Cheap petrol makes driving there surprisingly economical too

World of motoring
"Your car hire company may try to persuade you to upgrade to a better car, at wonderfully discounted rates. Bear in mind that sometimes this is offered because they have run short of the size of vehicle you have booked. Stick to your guns, and you may get a free upgrade."
Peter Upton

How to rent a car

You can wait to hire a car when you arrive at your destination, or book it from home before you leave.

If you plan to have a car for the entire duration of your stay, it makes a lot of sense to book from home. Then you have all the paperwork sorted in advance and the car will be waiting for you to pick up at your holiday airport. Booking from a major multinational car hire company at home actually often works out cheaper than going to a local outfit abroad, and it should also make it easier to sort out any problems if anything goes wrong.

If you're staying at a holiday resort you may just want to hire a car for a few days to explore the surrounding area. In this case there are usually plenty of rental outlets which may offer good deals on short term car hire. Bear in mind that in smaller resorts, such as the Greek islands, cars can be in short supply at peak periods and booking in advance is recommended to ensure you won't be disappointed.

There are often cheap weekly packages on offer so check you don't end up paying more by hiring a car for five days than you would for a whole week. Agencies that make their bread and butter hiring to business users may have attractive weekend deals.

Avoid the very cheapest deals. You may find yourself facing high insurance surcharges, and the seediest operators aren't above discovering mysterious damage once you've returned your car. Some apparently cheap packages may add on extra charges if you wish to have more than one named driver, or won't include an unlimited mileage.

Generally you will need a credit card to hire a car. That allows the rental company to keep your credit card details as a security against any damage caused. Be aware that if they do find damage, the first you know about it could be weeks later when you receive your credit card statement.

Some companies now take debit cards too, and smaller outfits may accept cash but will generally

HIRING A CAR

demand some extra security – such as your airline tickets – as a deposit against accident damage.

Particularly when renting in the United States, take care that the hire charge you are quoted is the inclusive rate. What is termed the 'base rental car rate' often turns out to attract a host of extra charges, including sales taxes, airport taxes and concession fees, which can inflate it by over a third.

When you pick up your car you will need to produce both parts of your photocard driving licence. In an emergency, try contacting the DVLA who should be able to confirm your licence details by phone or fax within office hours. Remember also that an International Driving Permit is not sufficient when hiring a car; the hirer will want to see your British driving licence as well.

If you have hired a car in the UK which you plan to take abroad, some rental companies operate a scheme that allows you to swap your car for a left-hand-drive model once you've crossed the Channel. In any case, you must inform your rental company if you intend taking one of its vehicles abroad.

Choosing the right car

Think about the sort of driving you're planning to do before booking a car. If you intend to cover short distances on minor roads on a holiday island, the smallest and cheapest car may be quite adequate. But if you're planning more ambitious journeys with a lot of motorway driving then it could be worth upgrading to a larger, more comfortable car. Hire cars in the US are generally bigger than at home, but due to the low price of petrol a larger model can still be cost-effective.

If heading to a hot climate, don't underestimate the benefit of air conditioning. Opening windows to try to cool down can be counterproductive when it's really scorching, as the inflow of hot air is both dehydrating and fatiguing. Don't worry if you see a small amount of water dripping from beneath an air-conditioned car when you park it – this is quite normal after a hot drive.

World of motoring
"If hiring a car in Canada or the US it is a false economy to hire a compact car. A full-size saloon is little more expensive but much more comfortable on a long journey. A 3.0-litre auto will still do 27-29mpg on petrol that costs a fraction of the price in the UK."
Mike Green

Choose a type of car suitable for your driving needs. On a Greek Island with no motorways, a small car like this Renault Twingo is quite adequate

WEST GATE CENTER

TEMP: 91F

Don't overlook how hot it can get in some holiday destinations during the summer. Hiring a car fitted with air conditioning can make a big difference to your comfort levels

Added extras

It's reassuring to know that your car is equipped to look after you if you have an accident. Confirm when making your booking if you want to have such features as airbags and anti-lock brakes.

Rental companies should be able to supply a child seat, but again it's worth checking when you book. These can work out expensive to hire, so despite the inconvenience it can pay to take along your own seat with your luggage.

If heading where snow is likely, it will also be necessary to specify whether you need a car equipped with snow tyres.

Disabled drivers may need to book well in advance to obtain a car fitted with hand controls. Car hire companies in America are usually well equipped in this respect, but be prepared to have to get the hang of controls which differ from those you are used to in the UK. It can be advisable to deal directly with the hire company at your destination to ensure there is no confusion over your requirements.

Make sure your hire car includes a recovery service in the event of a breakdown. If you're planning to drive into remote areas, particularly in the US, it can make sense to hire a mobile phone in case you need to call for assistance. Most car hire companies rent these cheaply, although if you do use them the actual call time is expensive.

Don't neglect to keep an eye on the oil, screenwash and tyre pressures just because it's a hire car. Follow the maintenance advice given on page 15.

Most hire cars come supplied with a map but it's normally chosen for cheapness rather than clarity or accuracy. Buying a decent road map at the outset of your journey can save endless frustrating wrong turns and hold ups.

Specify in advance if you need to book a child seat along with your rental car. Alternatively, you may feel happier taking your own seat with you

HIRING A CAR

Age limits

Statistically, young drivers have a much higher risk of being involved in a road accident. From age 25 the graph starts to flatten out, before rising again at retirement age. Motor insurance premiums follow these figures closely (as any 19-year old who tries to insure a sports car will find out), and car rental companies also use them as a guide to whom they consider desirable customers. Anyone under 21 will find it difficult to hire a car. From 21 to 25, some companies may decline to accept your custom, depending on where you want to hire a car, and others may impose a surcharge.

Drivers aged over 70 years may encounter similar problems, which can be galling if you have several decades of blemish-free motoring behind you. The answer is to shop around, as some major rental companies do not discriminate against elderly drivers.

Crossing borders

Always discuss with your rental company beforehand if you intend to cross a border in your hire car. In most cases this won't be a problem. US rental outfits are generally relaxed about you taking their car to Canada, but less happy about letting you pop over to Mexico. Most European outfits will let you wander throughout the EU, but may draw the line at some Eastern European countries. Under current EU regulations, EU nationals are not allowed to drive a car rented outside the EU into EU territory.

One-way rentals are a useful way of extending the amount of ground you can cover when time is limited. Instead of picking up and returning the car at the same site, you can arrange to pick it up from one place and return it to another. So rather than, for instance, flying into Los Angeles, renting a car for a fortnight and returning it there before you leave, you could arrange to pick up the car in LA and leave it in Seattle, flying home from there. Bear in mind that there is usually a surcharge if you intend to leave the car at a different site.

World of motoring
"Travel with soft bags in case the Megane Scenic you thought you had hired for your family of five turns out to be an Alfa Romeo saloon with an odd, non-suitcase-shaped boot! If you do think luggage is going to be a problem, then specify a roof box at the time you hire your car."
Bruce Harrison

Arranging insurance when you hire a car can be a confusing business, but it pays to read the small print before signing to ensure you are adquately covered – and that you aren't paying out for insurance you don't need

Hire car insurance

Arranging hire car insurance is a complicated, confusing and expensive business. Even when you believe you have booked comprehensive cover, you may be met at the airport hire counter with an invitation to upgrade to a series of expensive extras. Insurance is couched in an arcane series of legal terms and initials seemingly designed to bewilder the customer further.

The local legal minimum of third party or liability insurance should be included in the basic rental price and is a legal requirement in most countries. It should cover loss and damage caused to other persons, including passengers in your hire car.

Collision Damage Waiver (CDW) covers damage caused to the hire car, and is important to have if you don't want to risk an enormous bill if you have a crash. It may not include theft, in which case you will also need Theft Protection (TP) which should cover theft of the vehicle or its accessories.

In the United States, CDW is often called Loss Damage Waiver (LDW), in which case it should also cover theft as well as 'loss of use'. If you do not have LDW and the car is damaged, the rental company may expect you to pay for the rental fees lost while the car is off the road being repaired.

Even after taking out CDW or LDW, you could still find yourself liable for a hefty bill if you return the car damaged, depending on the size of the excess. If the excess is $500, this means that you have to pay for the first $500 of repairs.

You may be able to pay an Excess Reduction (ER) fee (sometimes called Super CDW) to lower the

World of motoring
"Hire companies in the US hate cash! If you haven't got a credit card you could find yourself having to hand over $1500 (£860) before being allowed to hire a car. This is more than some people spend in a fortnight!"
Les Spedding

HIRING A CAR

amount of excess. But take care, as this can be expensive. Even if you have a zero excess, you may still have to pay for damage to windscreen or tyres.

Check whether your insurance covers you to drive on gravel roads. Many companies specifically exclude this, others include a clause that makes the driver liable for any damage caused to the underbody of the vehicle. It's important to be sure, especially if you're hiring a holiday villa which is at the end of a long unmade road. Where driving on gravel roads is essential, you may be able to arrange to pay extra to top up the cover.

In the US, where civil litigation is common, you should strongly consider taking out extra cover against injured third parties suing you for damages. This is called Supplementary Liability Insurance (SLI), or Extended Protection (EP), and you should take out at least $1m of cover for peace of mind.

Rental companies often offer their own special insurance packages, labelled with unhelpful tags such as VIP, Gold, or Executive. Don't sign up until you're sure you understand exactly what's on offer.

Make sure you're not paying for insurance cover you already have. Check to see if your motor insurance policy, travel insurance, or credit card gives you any degree of cover. For instance, travel insurance may cover theft of personal possessions from the car and legal liability. Travel insurance often specifically excludes valuables left in an unattended car, but you may be able to cover these under your home insurance policy.

Annual hire car insurance is available from some credit card companies, but check this is suitable for your needs as not all hire companies are prepared to rent vehicles without their own insurance cover.

Opting for a belt-and-braces insurance package may be expensive, especially for something that you hope never actually to use. But the last thing you want when on holiday is to be worrying about whether you would be properly covered if you had a crash.

World of motoring
"Watch out for extra costs involved with car hire. I booked a pre-paid hire car with inclusive collision damage waiver from Barcelona airport. On reaching the head of the queue at the car hire desk I was informed that there was a €600 (£420) excess. I was offered super collision damage waiver at an extra cost of €11 (£8) per day which would reduce the excess to zero."
Lyn Heslop

Look for damage on your car when picking it up, and make sure any you find is clearly marked on the rental agreement. Check tyres are legal too, especially when hiring from a low-cost local outfit

World of motoring
"Always check the tyres and wheel trims on your hire car. Despite claims that insurance is all-inclusive, it does not cover tyres and trims. If you notice any damage, speak to a hire car representative before you drive away from the airport and ask that the damage is noted on the hire contract."
Les Spedding

Collecting your car

You can be met by long queues at airport car hire booths. A pre-registration service (whereby all your details are already entered into the system so all you need to do is sign and collect the keys) can speed up the process if it is available. If flying in late at night, check that the hire desk will still be open. You may be asked to pay a small fee for out-of-hours service.

On picking up your car always take some time to walk round it and inspect it for existing damage, particularly scratches, scuffed wheels, and cracked windscreen or headlamps. This damage should be marked on your hire paperwork. If not, make sure it is added to the agreement before driving off, or you could find yourself paying for damage you haven't caused when you return the car.

Before driving off, ask someone from the hire firm to show you where all the controls are and how they operate. Make sure the seat belts work too.

HIRING A CAR

Returning your car

Most rental companies charge by the day, so if you return your car late you may have to pay for a whole extra day's rental. But don't feel you have to break speed limits to get back to the hire depot if you're running a few minutes late – most companies allow at least one hour's grace before levying an extra charge.

Remember to top up your petrol tank before returning your car. If the rental company has to refill the tank it will charge you for fuel at an exorbitant rate. Many rental companies offer the option of purchasing the full tank of fuel that the car comes with, so you can return it empty at no extra cost. This can be handy if you know time is going to be tight when you return the car, but otherwise you'll be wasting money for every drop of fuel you leave in the tank.

Stories abound of customers dropping off their hire car apparently undamaged only to later find themselves billed for repair work. Some companies automatically charge a set sum – typically £100 – for any damage, even a scuffed hub cap. You should get the extent and nature of any damage agreed in writing when you return the car, so if you later feel you are being overcharged you can use this to argue for a refund. Take some photographs of any damage to act as extra ammunition.

Whether the car is damaged or not, ideally you should try to have it checked and passed by the rental company when you return it to avoid any possible scope for misunderstanding.

Unfortunately, complaints over charges for alleged damage to hire cars are all too common. One survey found that more than 30 per cent of car rentals at airports in the US resulted in a dispute. One advantage of booking your hire car through a UK hire company is that they will be covered by the British Vehicle Rental and Leasing Association code, which gives you access to its conciliation service.

Remember to fill up your hire car with fuel before returning it. If you don't, the rental company will do it for you and charge you at an inflated rate

World of motoring

A survey carried out by *Holiday Which?* put 60 hire cars on Rhodes and the Costa Blanca through a mechanical inspection and found that only four would pass the British MOT test. However, cars from multinational hire companies were generally in better shape than those from local outfits

Left-hand-drive

When you hire a car in a country where traffic drives on the right it will of course be left-hand-drive. If you've never driven abroad before, this may seem an extra difficulty to have to master. In fact, it actually makes driving abroad a lot easier than if you were in your own right-hand-drive car. In a left-hand-drive car, driving on the right side of the road comes more naturally, you acclimatise to driving on the right more quickly and are less likely to make mistakes when positioning your car on the road.

If you've never driven a left-hand-drive car before, you'll be relieved to know that not everything is back to front. The pedals are still in the same position: clutch on the left, brake in the middle and accelerator on the right. The position of indicator, headlamp and wiper stalks should also be the same as they would be in the UK (indicators and headlamps controlled by the left stalk, wipers by the right). Japanese cars used to follow the opposite pattern but have mostly adopted the European style nowadays, leaving just a handful of other Far-Eastern manufacturers using the opposite pattern.

For the first few days a left-hand-drive car does feel unfamiliar. It's harder to judge how close you are to

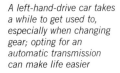

A left-hand-drive car takes a while to get used to, especially when changing gear; opting for an automatic transmission can make life easier

HIRING A CAR

overtaking parked vehicles until you get a feel for the
width of the car.

Having a gear stick on your right can feel awkward
at first, resulting in poorly co-ordinated gear changes.
Don't despair if you find yourself putting your left
hand into the driver's door pocket when you by habit
reach for where your brain tells you the gear stick
should be.

Looking over your right shoulder instead of your left
in order to see behind when reversing can also feel
profoundly unnatural. But most people find that after
the first few days, driving a left-hand-drive car
becomes second nature.

Your hire car may differ from your own car back
home in a few other ways. Many American models
have a foot-operated parking brake instead of a
handbrake. To engage the parking brake, push down
this pedal. When you release it, the brake stays on.
To disengage the parking brake, you may need to
pull a lever mounted under the dashboard, or in
some cars press the foot pedal again.

Foot-operated parking brakes are a dubious benefit
as they remove the main advantage of a handbrake,
which is that you can hold the car stationary while
moving your foot from the brake pedal to the
accelerator (this is less of a drawback on cars with
automatic gearboxes, which is why foot-operated
parking brakes are so common in the US).

Cruise control is also more common in America
than it is here. Using cruise control, the driver can
set a speed which is then maintained automatically
until the system is switched off or overridden by
pressing the accelerator or brake pedal. Cruise
control can be a real benefit when covering long
distances on uncrowded highways, allowing you to
maintain a safe speed with no risk of creeping over
the speed limit. But don't use cruise control in the
wet or when traffic is heavy, and look out in Belgium
for signs prohibiting its use on some roads.

Automatic transmissions are easy to use. Remember that the gear shift must be in Park to start the car, and that it will start creeping forward when you engage Drive

World of motoring
"If you can drive an auto, then hire an auto. It allows you to concentrate 100% on the road."
Bruce Harrison

Driving an automatic

Automatic transmissions are much more popular in the US, accounting for around 85 per cent of new car sales compared with under 15 per cent in Europe.

Automatic cars are well suited to the long, straight highways of America. More pertinent perhaps is that with their fuel costing just a third of European prices, Americans can afford to overlook the higher fuel consumption of their automatics. When hiring a car in the States you will almost certainly get an auto, and even if you specifically ask for a manual (called a *stick-shift*) you may find one isn't available.

Driving an automatic has the advantage of reducing the need for right-handed gear changing, which most British drivers find slightly awkward when switching to a left-hand-drive car.

If you've never driven an automatic car before, these hints may be useful:

♦ Ensure the gear shift is in Park and your foot is firmly on the brake pedal before trying to start the ignition. Most autos are designed not to start unless these precautions are taken

♦ When you are ready to drive away, move the lever out of Park and into Drive. To do this you will need to push down the security button mounted on the gear lever. You also need to press this button when shifting into Reverse. Hold the car on the brake as the car will automatically begin to creep forward once Drive is engaged

♦ Do not use your left foot for braking when driving an automatic. It would be too easy to confuse which foot you should be using if you have to brake in an emergency

♦ When coming to a brief halt, for instance at traffic lights, there is no need to move the gear shift out of Drive. But if stopped for more than a few seconds you should use the parking brake to immobilise the car (if you were hit from behind by another car without the parking brake on, you would risk being pushed out into oncoming traffic)

◆ If you need to accelerate quickly while in Drive, for instance to overtake another vehicle, press down firmly on the accelerator. This will cause the gearbox to kick down to a lower gear

◆ On steep downhill sections engage a lower gear manually to give extra engine braking. Which gear you use depends on how many the car has – some cheaper US hire cars only have three-speed 'boxes. Bottom gear is marked L (for low) and intermediate gears are numbered. You can also select a lower gear to give extra control when overtaking or cornering, or when climbing uphill to stop the gearbox 'hunting' – continually changing gear as it searches for the right ratio

◆ On stopping the car at the end of the journey, engage the parking brake and put the gear shift into Park before switching off the ignition.

Hiring a motorbike

The most sensible of us have been known to throw all caution to the wind when on holiday, and few temptations are potentially more perilous than hiring a motorbike. Hopping on a scooter in the Greek Islands while wearing sandals, shorts and a t-shirt is asking for trouble, but each year many British holidaymakers do just this and end up badly – sometimes fatally – injured. Unless you are already an experienced biker, a foreign country is no place to start exploring the delights of motoring on two wheels.

Motorbike hire is especially popular in exotic locations such as Thailand and Goa in India – which are precisely where the dangers on the road are greatest. Bikes there may be in poor condition, local roads treacherous and driving standards far below what we're used to in the West. Hire shops may not

It is sometimes necessary to override an automatic transmission and select a lower gear manually - for instance, when needing extra engine braking on a steep downhill gradient

99

World of motoring
"Riding a borrowed bike in Kuta, Bali, I was stopped by traffic police at a road check. I was fined IDR50,000 (£3.50) as I was not able to produce the STNK, which is proof of the owner's identity (I later discovered it was with me all along, stored in the bike's key ring wallet)."
Tim Dishman

Hiring a motorbike can be enjoyable abroad, but only for experienced riders. Always wear a helmet, no matter what local bikers do

supply helmets (whether or not their use is compulsory) with the consequence that a relatively minor accident can result in serious injury. Always insist on wearing a helmet, no matter how strenuously the hire salesman tells you one isn't needed. Better still, take your own helmet which you know is undamaged and conforms to international standards, as well as some basic protective clothing. And don't try to make a false economy by hiring one underpowered moped for two to share – it won't feel stable and you won't be safe.

For more experienced bikers, hiring a bike abroad takes on a different complexion. It can form the basis of an unusual and highly entertaining holiday. Look out for tours organised in places like India that give you all the fun of riding through an exotic country with none of the hassle of organising the trip yourself.

Hiring a motorhome

A motorhome offers a convenient and enjoyable way to explore a country. You have everything you need on board in a self-contained unit that includes kitchen, bathroom, sleeping and dining quarters, combined with the freedom to go wherever you like.

Motorhome holidays are particularly popular in the US. Recreational vehicles, or RVs, as they are known there, are a common sight. Some American RVs are vast machines, and you'll even encounter owners towing their everyday car along behind them.

A driver accustomed to driving a small hatchback may find the sheer size of a motorhome disconcerting, but it doesn't present any special driving problems. Power steering takes the strain out of manoeuvring, while large rectangular door mirrors give a clear field of view down each side. Driving a motorhome is certainly less of a challenge than towing a caravan for the first time.

Having said that, it's not a good idea to leap into a motorhome straight off the plane when you're tired and concentration is at its lowest ebb. Many

HIRING A CAR

motorhome suppliers insist that drivers don't take to the road until the day after they arrive.

The larger dimensions of a motorhome take a while to get accustomed to, although if you're driving in America the generous road widths and parking lots make manoeuvring a motorhome easier than it is in Europe. Once you're used to it, the high vantage point of a motorhome's cab adds an enjoyable extra dimension to motoring, opening up wide views of the surrounding landscape.

Make sure you know exactly how big your vehicle is: it's a good idea to jot the height and width on a piece of paper and attach it to the sun visor. Beware of car parks that have a barrier set too low for you to creep under when you're in a vehicle 10ft or more in height. Single track roads are also worth steering clear of, at least until you are confident at reversing. If you do get into a tight spot, folding the door mirrors flat may help you squeeze through.

Don't expect much more than 15mpg from a big American RV (although of course the lower petrol prices in the US are a compensation). Make sure you are comprehensively insured. It's worth paying more to get your excess reduced, because it's easy to pick up a knock in such a large vehicle when you're not used to driving one.

Equipped with everything you need – including the kitchen sink – renting a motorhome can be the ideal way to go exploring

EXTREME
CONDITIONS

It's sometimes hard to believe it, but here in Britain we have a particularly mild, gentle climate and few natural hazards. We never experience the sort of heat which can fry an egg on your car bonnet or the arctic cold that freezes an engine solid. We don't have to worry about running into a tornado on the way to work, or losing our way in a sandstorm coming back from the supermarket.

But you don't have to go far beyond these shores to experience some pretty serious natural hazards. When driving abroad, particularly in more out of the way areas, it's important to be on the alert for hazards that aren't familiar back home. Recognise that there are times, places and conditions when it simply isn't safe to be on the road, no matter how urgent your journey seems, and always heed the advice of local people about travelling conditions.

103

Snow, ice and temperatures as low as minus 30C characterise the Scandinavian winter, presenting some challenging driving conditions for motorists

Winter driving tips

- ◆ Get your antifreeze and battery checked before leaving home. Flat batteries are the main cause of breakdowns in winter
- ◆ Increase screenwash concentration to stop your windscreen washer freezing in extremely low temperatures
- ◆ Inspect tyres to ensure they have plenty of tread
- ◆ Carry some windscreen de-icer, a scraper, and a brush for sweeping snow off the car
- ◆ Never start driving before your car is completely defrosted. Driving while peering through a tiny hole in an icy windscreen is dangerous and illegal. Clear ice from lights and number plates too
- ◆ Carry snowchains and plenty of warm clothes
- ◆ Use your headlights in poor light, and switch on foglamps when visibility is less than 100 metres

Driving in winter

Heavy snowfall is rare in the UK, particularly in the south. That means British drivers don't get much opportunity to gain experience in coping with freezing conditions. When snow does fall, it invariably brings chaos to the roads.

It's a different story across much of Europe and North America. In Scandinavia, for instance, motorists take winter in their stride. At the first snowfall they routinely swap their summer tyres for studded winter tyres. These give a surprising amount of grip even on the most icy surfaces. I've driven a car wearing studded tyres on a frozen lake so slippery that I found it difficult to stand up when I got out of the car.

Studded tyres aren't suitable for use on snow-free roads, though. In Central Europe, where snow cover is less continuous but still frequently encountered in most winters, many motorists fit winter tyres when the weather worsens. Although these don't incorporate studs, they do have tread specially designed to grip in slippery conditions. The advantage of winter tyres is that they can be used on dry tarmac - although in these conditions they don't provide quite as much grip as normal tyres, and their chunky treads generate a little more road noise. If you're planning to make frequent trips abroad in winter, it might make sense to consider investing in a set of winter tyres.

Snow chains

On snow-covered roads, whether or not you have winter tyres you will need a pair of snow chains. In the Alps it's a legal requirement to carry a set in your car during winter and fit them when conditions demand. This requirement is indicated by a circular blue sign showing a tyre fitted with a snow chain.

Snow chains fit to the car's driven wheels, enabling them to bite into the snow and grip instead of spinning uselessly. You can hire chains from some ski shops and motoring organisations, but if you plan to use them more than once then it can be worth buying a set. They might even come in handy on the odd snowbound day back home. Don't wait until you're in the mountains and need a set urgently.

World of motoring

In some American states an R code indicates when snow chains must be used:

R1 Snow tyres or snow chains must be used

R2 All 2WD cars must use snow chains and 4WD cars must carry chains

R3 All cars must fit snow chains

There are often control points to check compliance with these rules. You may come across snow chain fitters at lay-bys who will put your chains on your car for you for a fee

It is compulsory to carry snow chains wherever you see this blue sign

EXTREME CONDITIONS

World of motoring
"On holiday in Madeira, I hired a car to explore the hilly western side of the island. At the top of the hills it suddenly became foggy, with vision reduced to ten metres. I then discovered that locals drive with hazard lights on as well as their fog lights. It seemed a good idea, and overall I was impressed by the standard of driving on the island."
Ivan Marner

Study the instructions on the snow chains carefully and if you're uncertain how to fit them, ask for a demonstration when you buy the chains. They must be exactly the right size for the tyres fitted to your car. Most snowchains are easy to fit, and the more convenient types can be fitted without having to move the car. You don't need to alter the tyre pressures when using snowchains. Do practice putting them on before you need to use them in earnest. Carry a stout pair of gloves to wear when fitting them.

Drive extra cautiously for the first few miles after fitting snow chains – if you hear any clanking sounds, it probably means one of the chains is loose and needs retensioning. In any case you shouldn't exceed 30mph when using snowchains.

Don't let the extra grip snow chains provide give a false sense of security. Leave extra stopping distances and brake and accelerate as smoothly as possible.

Check the chains frequently and do not use chains that are excessively worn or which have a broken link. If they break during use they can cause considerable damage.

Winter lighting
Along with snow and ice, winter brings poor visibility. Don't wait to be the last to switch on your headlamps. In Poland it's a legal requirement to use dipped headlamps day and night from October to February, while Scandinavian countries and some Canadian provinces insist on using dipped lights all year round.

Switch on fog lamps if visibility falls below 100 metres. Remember that your rear fog lamps are designed to alert a following vehicle to your presence. Keeping them switched on when in a stream of closely packed traffic will simply dazzle and irritate the driver behind you. Fog lamps can also mask your brake lamps, adding to and not reducing danger when used unnecessarily.

Starting on ice

Driving on snow and ice demands some special techniques. Surprisingly, what makes roads slippery in freezing conditions is not ice, but water. As a tyre rolls over a frozen surface, it melts the uppermost layer of ice. This turns to water, forming a film between the tread of the tyre and the ice. The tyre slides on this film of water, in much the same way as it does when aquaplaning on a puddle in the road.

Simply getting away from a standstill can be tricky in freezing conditions, especially if you're trying to pull away uphill. Apply too much throttle and the driven wheels will spin frantically with no forward motion.

This is where four-wheel-drive comes into its own. With the driving force distributed between four wheels instead of two, wheelspin is much more easily avoided. Traction control, now increasingly fitted, gives two-wheel-drive cars a similar advantage. Traction control works by automatically cutting the power or applying the brake to a driven wheel when it starts to spin, giving it a chance to regain grip.

If your car lacks either four-wheel-drive or traction control, the secret of moving off on a slippery surface is to engage a higher gear than normal – second or even third. Bring the clutch up until you feel it begin to bite, then gently rev the engine until you feel the car start to move. Then you can gradually let out the clutch the whole way and apply more power.

Moving off on a frozen surface needs delicate throttle control to avoid wheelspin; starting in second gear usually helps

World of motoring

"In Serbia it is an offence to drive with fog lamps or driving lamps illuminated unless there is fog with reduced visibility. I was asked to pay a 1000 Dinar (£10) fine, but was excused after explaining that I am a volunteer driver for an Aid Agency."
Harry Wilby

Braking distances are greatly increased on ice. Anti-lock brakes help (although they can't work miracles) and they allow you to steer and brake at the same time

Stopping on ice

If getting moving poses a problem on a slippery surface, so does coming to a halt. Just as you need a very progressive application of the throttle when moving off, so you must be very gentle with the brakes to stop. Try to imagine that you're driving barefoot and the brake pedal is covered in tin tacks. Press very gently at first, gradually increase the braking effort, then ease off as you come to a halt. If you feel the wheels begin to slip, ease off the pedal until the wheels regain traction then reapply the brakes.

If you stamp on the brake pedal in an emergency when driving on ice, the wheels will instantly stop rotating. Locked up wheels provide very little braking effort on a slippery surface so your car will continue to slide inexorably towards the object you're hoping to avoid.

To prevent this, most modern cars are fitted with anti-lock brakes (often called ABS). ABS works by sensing when the wheels are on the verge of locking up under braking. The car's electronics then take over, releasing the brake until the wheel begins to roll, then reapplying it until the wheel starts to lock up again. This cycle is repeated many times every second.

Drivers often think the primary purpose of ABS is to reduce stopping distances in an emergency, but this isn't the whole story. In slippery situations ABS does give a shorter stopping distance than a car with locked up wheels. But even ABS can't work miracles on snow or ice. You need to allow a much longer stopping distance than you would if braking on dry tarmac.

The real advantage of ABS is that it allows the driver to retain control of the steering under emergency braking. Locked up tyres can't steer; if you slam on the brakes and start to slide, moving the steering wheel has absolutely no effect on your direction of travel.

With ABS, because the wheels don't lock up you can still steer, which gives you a fighting chance of avoiding the object you've braked to avoid. What you need to do is to keep your foot pressed hard on the brake pedal so the ABS continues to activate while you gently steer a safe path round the obstacle. Depressing the clutch can help the tyres find a little extra grip.

If your car is not fitted with ABS then you have to mimic the action of ABS to slow it down. When you feel the wheels lock up under braking, lift off the brake pedal to let them start rolling again, then reapply the brakes. Lifting off the brake pedal also allows you to regain control of the steering, giving you an opportunity to steer round the obstacle ahead. Needless to say, making yourself take your foot off the brake as you slide towards an obstacle isn't the most natural reaction, and this is a driving technique which really needs practise at a skid pan to master.

Warning of the risk of ice on the road, this sign is widely used throughout Europe, and gives a useful indication of where extra care may be needed in cold weather

Anticipation and a smooth driving style are vital to avoid skidding on snow

Controlling slides

The most common slide in a front-wheel-drive car is caused when the front wheels lose grip. You turn the steering wheel on the approach to a bend but nothing happens. The car continues to career straight on, no matter how much steering lock you apply.

If this starts to happen, immediately come off the accelerator. This throws the weight balance of the car forwards and helps the front wheels find more grip. Gently wind off some of the steering lock you have applied. As the wheels straighten up you should feel them start to bite again, and you can carefully steer the car back on course. It also helps to disengage the clutch.

A rear-wheel skid can be more dramatic and if not controlled may develop into a spin. What happens is that the rear wheels lose grip, usually because the car has been thrown off balance by lifting off the power or braking harshly in the middle of the bend. The rear of the car then starts to slide round. To correct this, lift off the accelerator and brake pedals, and steer back in the direction you want to head. You may need to wind on more steering lock to bring the tail of the car back in line, but try not to overcorrect or it can pendulum right back in the opposite direction.

This sounds complicated but most drivers will correct a skid instinctively: the important thing is not to panic, and to keep looking in the direction you want to travel, not towards the obstacle you're afraid you might hit.

No matter how much good advice you read on the subject, real confidence in driving on snow and ice can only come with practice, and on the UK's largely snow-free roads we get little opportunity to acquire the necessary skills. Some advanced driving courses include skid pan training which can give invaluable experience in dealing with slides. These courses are becoming increasingly popular among organisations which run company cars, so if your firm offers you

Take great care on cobbled streets, still common in many villages in France. This type of surface is treacherous when damp and it's deceptively easy to skid

EXTREME CONDITIONS

the chance to go on a course, take it.

The bottom line of dealing with skids is not to get into one in the first place. Skids are not caused by bad road conditions, they are caused by driving too quickly for those conditions. In poor weather you must greatly increase your stopping distance, so if the vehicle in front of you stops unexpectedly you have plenty of space in which to brake gently to a halt without skidding. On approaching a bend you must anticipate the lack of grip on an icy road, slow right down, select a low gear well in advance, and be gentle and progressive in your use of the steering, accelerator and brakes.

As always, the secret of safe driving on snow and ice is using your common sense to stay out of trouble in the first place – not relying on your reactions to get you out of a tricky situation.

There's no substitute for experience when trying to correct a slide, and a session on the skid pan can boost your confidence enormously

Alpine driving

Drivers heading for the more scenic parts of Europe soon find themselves tackling some pretty mountainous terrain. This requires driving techniques not often called upon in Britain. There are few classified roads here that get to over 2,000ft (600m); compare this with France, where the highest *col* or mountain pass, the Col de Restefond, reaches 9,193ft (2,082m).

In mountainous areas rapid changes in altitude, steep slopes and narrow roads all combine to give tricky driving conditions. The higher you go the colder it gets. To see this point dramatically illustrated, go to the Sierra Nevada mountains of southern Spain. While skiers tackle the slopes 3,000 metres above sea level, just 25 miles away on the Costa del Sol it can be warm enough to sunbathe.

Freezing conditions are most dangerous when they are unexpected. It may be warm and sunny as you set off from the valley floor, but as you gain height conditions can deteriorate with startling speed. Keep an eye on the outside temperature gauge if your car has one. Take special care where the road passes under shadows cast by trees or rocks, as these could harbour icy patches which haven't had a chance to melt in the sun. When driving over an icy surface the steering may feel unusually light and there can be a drop in tyre noise. Gently lift off the accelerator to slow the car but avoid braking which could cause a loss of control.

Higher passes are often blocked completely during the winter months. When there is snow on the ground it makes sense to stick to major roads which are the first to be cleared by snow ploughs. Make

Always give way to post office vehicles in Switzerland on roads marked with this blue rectangle showing a yellow horn. Some Swiss roads are one way, but at certain times of day only. Pay careful attention to the signs at each end of the road which advise when the priority changes

EXTREME CONDITIONS

sure you have a good map which clearly marks the heights of mountain passes and shows the time of year when they are likely to be closed. If in doubt, stop and seek local advice.

If you do encounter snow, don't wait to get into difficulty but pull over and fit snow chains at the first opportunity.

Whatever the weather, alpine passes should be tackled with care. These roads can provide truly spectacular driving. The sense of natural drama is enthralling as you follow a snaking road up from the lushness of an alpine valley, into thick pine forests which are gradually replaced by sparser, stunted vegetation and scree until you emerge in the bleak and inhospitable world above the snow line. Finally, you crest the pass and a whole new vista unfolds.

Tackling an alpine pass is probably the toughest job you'll ever ask your car to do. Grinding slowly uphill, often at full throttle in a low gear, generates a lot of engine heat without a rapid flow of cooling air through the radiator to dissipate it. Engine power is also significantly reduced the higher you climb. If your car has any problems with its cooling system this is when they will come to light.

Keep a watchful eye on the engine temperature gauge. If it starts to creep upwards, putting the heater on full blast can help provide extra cooling, although you'll need to open the windows to avoid roasting. If this doesn't do the trick, pull over and let the engine cool down. Overheating is particularly likely to occur if you are towing, which puts a lot of extra strain on the engine.

Never pour cold water into a radiator that has boiled over or you run the risk of cracking it.

On the way back down it's the brakes which take the strain. Modern cars have disc brakes which are not prone to fade even under heavy use, but if your brake pads or discs are worn then you may start to experience fade. The brake pedal will need to be pressed harder to achieve the same rate of braking

These picturesque Swiss scenes encapsulate the drama of alpine driving; but great care is needed on roads that are often steep, narrow and winding

Allow plenty of time for your journey in mountainous regions, where winding roads give few overtaking opportunities and progress can sometimes be slow

and will feel wooden and unresponsive. You may also notice an acrid burning smell from overheating brake pads. If you do experience these symptoms, pull in at the earliest opportunity and wait for the brakes to cool down completely before continuing.

To reduce the work the brakes have to do always engage a lower gear when tackling a long descent. This maximises the effect of engine braking and gives you more control over your vehicle.

When driving in the mountains, bear in mind that all that twisting and climbing takes time. You can easily spend the best part of a morning crossing a pass, then look at the map and be amazed when you see how little distance you've covered. Driving in the mountains is something to do for the enjoyment of the trip – if you're trying to cover a lot of miles you're better off sticking to major routes which tunnel through or bypass mountain ranges much more efficiently.

If you don't have a great head for heights, it may be better to avoid small alpine roads altogether. Driving along a narrow mountain road can be unnerving, especially in an unfamiliar left-hand-drive hire car. Oncoming drivers will expect you to pull well over to the right to let them through, regardless of the precipice inches away from your wheels.

Progress can be particularly slow on single-track roads which wind apparently endlessly through the hills. Particular care is needed here. After half an hour or so of negotiating blind bends without meeting another vehicle it's easy to forget that you may have to stop in a hurry. Keep looking well ahead and across valleys when the opportunity arises. You can often spot oncoming vehicles when they are some distance away, and so be prepared to stop.

On very twisting roads you may have limited vision of the road ahead, so keep your eyes and ears open. Opening the window can give advanced warning by letting you hear the approach of a vehicle before you see it. In some areas the locals sound their horn before each blind bend, apparently in the belief that this makes it safe for them to take the bend without slowing down. So if you hear a horn, slow right down and be prepared to give way.

On a single track road it's easy to forget that you are still in theory driving on the right. When you meet another vehicle you have to consciously overcome an automatic reaction to pull to the left to let it pass.

Make note of passing places as you go by them, so if there's no room to squeeze past an oncoming vehicle you'll know how far you have to back up to let it by. Keep an eye on your rear view mirror too. Local drivers who are familiar with this sort of road will invariably want to go faster so pull over and let them overtake when you get the chance.

There's a general rule on mountain roads that drivers going downhill should give way to vehicles coming uphill. In many countries this is backed by the law, although in Austria the vehicle that finds it easiest to stop is the one that must give way. Whatever the rule of the road, never expect the other driver to give way. It's always quicker, easier and less stressful to give way when you get the chance rather than get involved in a stand-off with another driver – especially when as a foreigner you're not familiar with the local etiquette.

Look out for unusual hazards when driving off the beaten track; flocks of sheep or goats like this are often encountered in the mountains of Greece

Never drive into standing water unless you are absolutely certain it isn't too deep for safety

World of motoring

"In Florida, whenever your windscreen wipers are on, by law your headlights must be on too. This is especially important as when it does rain it can come down inches at a time."
Clare Reeves

Rain and floods

We're no strangers to heavy rain and floods in Britain. But here we tend to get plenty of warning, with floods following a period of persistent rainfall.

In many countries, particularly those that are normally hot and dry, floods can arise much more rapidly. There's less vegetation to soak up rain water and drainage systems are often inadequate. A short sharp cloudburst can result in roads running knee-deep in water.

Never attempt to drive through standing water unless you are certain how deep it is. Watch someone else make the attempt first, or wade through to assess the depth. Be sure you know how high from the ground your car's engine air intake is. This is situated quite low down on some models and if water is sucked into the engine it will cause serious damage.

If you decide to tackle the flood, drive through at a

slow but steady speed in bottom gear. Keep up the engine revs, slipping the clutch if necessary. Once out the other side, apply the brakes a few times to dry them out.

Rainfall in hot countries can bring further hazards. Just as snow in the UK causes chaos, drivers who aren't used to wet roads can easily be caught out. Leave extra space around your vehicle to allow for other drivers travelling too fast for the conditions. Dry roads accumulate a film of grease and rubber, which turns into an oily slick when wet, so the first rain after a prolonged dry spell can make roads treacherous.

Aquaplaning

Puddles of water are a particular hazard on high speed roads and motorways where you are most likely to experience aquaplaning. This occurs when the tyres lose contact with the road and slide along the surface of the water. You may feel a tug at the steering wheel as you start to aquaplane, then the wheel will go strangely light.

Don't attempt to steer or brake which could cause you to lose control. Ease off the accelerator and as the car loses speed the wheels will regain contact with the road surface. Slow down in conditions where aquaplaning is likely, and read the contours of the road ahead to anticipate whether water may be accumulating in dips and hollows where you may not see it until it is too late, particularly at night.

World of motoring
"Although it's in the desert, it does occasionally rain in Dubai and at times the rain can be heavy. As it is not usually possible there to forecast rain, the drain covers are often closed to stop the entry of sand, and roads flood until they are opened."
Frank Smith

Torrential downpours are a feature of some climates, often accompanied by hail and strong winds. Slow down in the reduced visibility and if necessary pull over and wait for conditions to improve

Well-maintained gravel roads can provide a surprisingly smooth drive. But be careful when approaching dips where seasonal watercourses may break up the road surface

World of motoring

"When in tornado territory in the US, keep the car radio on and listen for warnings (and make sure you know where you are as these are given by county). I know from personal experience how terrifying a tornado can be when driving. The recommended procedure is to stop and find shelter in a shopping mall or building. Failing that, use an overpass bridge and get right up under the bridge as high as possible. Whatever you do, GET UNDER COVER."
John Kent

Gravel roads

In the UK we rarely drive on unmade roads. In fact, visitors to this country can be surprised that even our smallest country lanes are neatly tarmacked although they may see only a handful of vehicles each day.

In many countries it's much less usual for minor roads to be tarmacked. In Australia or South Africa, even quite important roads may be left with a gravel surface. These roads are generally graded and well maintained and can be comfortably traversed in a normal two-wheel-drive car. It is however important to modify your driving style when travelling on a loose gravel surface.

In Namibia most roads away from the handful of main routes are gravel. On one trip I covered hundreds of miles on them in a standard Toyota Corolla without incident – not even a puncture.

But I remember feeling a little apprehensive when I picked up the car from the hire depot. In the compound sat several cars and a minibus which had all been rolled and written off on gravel roads. I didn't ask if they just represented the latest toll of accidents, or whether they were kept there as a deliberate warning. Either way it was an effective reminder that gravel roads must always be treated with caution.

The problem is that these roads can be so smooth that they lull you into driving too fast. Then you come to a bend and find that you can't corner at anywhere near the same speed on gravel as you would on tarmac. Cornering on gravel is much like driving on snow. Unless you keep your speed down and avoid harsh braking, steering and acceleration, there is a danger that your car will start to slide. And with ditches or hummocks bordering the road it's likely that a car sliding sideways will tip and roll over.

So reduce your speed when driving on gravel, and keep a vigilant eye on the road ahead. Slow down well in advance of any potential hazard, so you can negotiate it at a safe speed.

Even high quality gravel roads can have patches of very rough going, especially where watercourses cross the road. These may only flow for a day or two each year, but when they do they deposit deep gravel and loose boulders to catch out the unwary. These dips may be signposted with warning triangles, but stay alert: the first five signs you encounter may indicate nothing more than minor depressions in the track; the sixth will precede a jagged ravine that has to be picked across at walking speed.

Corrugations can be a problem on less well maintained gravel tracks. The repeated passage of vehicles causes a series of undulations, like an endless succession of speed humps, to form along the track. Taken too slowly or too quickly, these send violent shudders through your vehicle, threatening to shake it and you to pieces. But it's usually possible to find a speed at which the wheels skim along the top of the humps to give a more comfortable ride. Again, don't forget that when you have to brake on

Driving in the desert can be dangerous, but the gravel roads of the Skeleton National Park in Namibia are a lot less intimidating than this sign on the gateway suggests

this sort of surface, stopping distances will be a lot longer than you may expect.

Overtaking on gravel tracks is a manoeuvre that demands special care. Vehicles throw up a plume of dust that makes it hard to get a clear view past. Flashing your headlamps can help alert a vehicle that you want to get by. You also need to slow down when you see a vehicle approaching and if possible get off the track to avoid a broken windscreen from flying gravel.

In desert regions, sand blowing across the road poses a special hazard. Soft sand saps engine power, slowing your car until it starts to bog down. In a standard two-wheel-drive vehicle you should be wary of trying to cross extended stretches of sand. Keep a steady momentum going and engage a lower gear to provide plenty of power. Try to avoid provoking wheelspin, which can cause the driven wheels to dig into the sand. Letting air (up to two-thirds of it) out of the tyres should improve grip, but make sure you pump them up again when you get back to firm ground – underinflated tyres can overheat with

Tackling gravel roads takes confidence, but they open the way to some of the most glorious scenery on the globe

EXTREME CONDITIONS

Dust is a big problem on gravel roads, seriously reducing visibility when you meet other traffic. Overtaking manoeuvres must be carried out with extreme caution

potentially serious consequences.

If you do bog down, try rocking the car to ease it out of the sand. Engage first gear, let the clutch in until the car starts to edge forward, then rapidly shift to reverse and do the same to edge the car backwards. Repeat this several times in quick succession and you may be able to develop sufficient momentum to break free. If this fails, try laying a carpet of brushwood or stones under the driving wheels to increase traction.

Always check your insurance position before driving a rented car on gravel roads. In some countries insurers may specifically exclude driving on gravel, or make the hirer liable for a higher excess for repair work caused on gravel.

But don't be put off driving on gravel roads. Once you're accustomed to them, they provide a thoroughly enjoyable driving experience, giving a feeling of being much closer to the landscape than when you are skimming over it insulated by a strip of tarmac.

In arid regions loose sand may blow across the road, threatening to bog down any two-wheel-drive vehicles that attempt to pass. Engage a low gear to cross patches of sand, and keep up momentum to avoid getting stuck

Serious desert driving needs considerable preparation and experience, as in the desert adventure can easily turn into tragedy

World of motoring

"If you plan to travel the outback – and there are many excellent reasons for doing so – make sure you know what you are doing. I've never forgotten the four overseas tourists found dead by their bogged vehicle. In the end the vehicle was extricated just by letting most of the air out of its tyres and driving it out. If only those tourists had known that little trick. . ."

Dr Anthony Wheeler

Desert driving

Driving across a desert is one of the last great motoring adventures. The classic Saharan crossing is sadly closed to foreigners at the moment due to civil unrest in Algeria and Morocco. It used to be possible – just about – to drive a standard two-wheel-drive vehicle across the major routes of the Sahara via romantic oasis towns such as Tamanghasset and Timbuktu. Canny travellers used to finance their trip by buying a car in France and selling it at a profit on arrival in Mali, where big Peugeot and Citroën estates are in great demand as taxis.

Although this route is closed there are still places the intrepid traveller can embark on an expedition across the desert. Australia has a number of classic desert routes. Some, such as the Birdsville Track, are usually passable for a two-wheel-drive vehicle; others, such as the Simpson Desert crossing, are much more serious undertakings for experienced desert drivers only, travelling in a convoy of 4x4s.

Never forget that the desert is an inhospitable and unforgiving place, where mistakes can be fatal. If you intend to drive anywhere in the desert it is essential to take the following precautions:

EXTREME CONDITIONS

- Ensure your vehicle is up to the job. Take local advice on whether a route is suitable for a standard car or if you'll need a 4x4 with low-ratio gearbox

- If you've never driven a 4x4 off-road before, take a training course to gain experience in the necessary techniques

- Have your vehicle serviced before leaving

- Take plenty of spare parts with you, and an extra spare wheel

- Drive a popular local vehicle rather than something exotic - you'll be more likely to find spares and someone who can fix it if it breaks

- Tell someone, such as the local police, where you're going and when you expect to arrive there

- Travel in convoy on more difficult sections

- Carry a radio in case you need to call for help

- Take plenty of jerrycans of spare fuel, or better still fit a long-range fuel tank. Remember your fuel consumption will be much higher when travelling in low ratio in a four-wheel-drive vehicle

- Take sand ladders and a spade in case you get bogged down

- Always carry an adequate supply of water – at least five litres per person per day.

- If you do break down, it's vital to resist the temptation to walk in search of help. The safest course of action is to stay with your vehicle, rig up some shade and wait for help to arrive.

Some areas are out of bounds, even to off-roaders! Never forget your responsibility to the environment when driving in more remote areas – desert habitats are more fragile than they look and can take decades to recover if disturbed

Crowded roads, badly maintained vehicles, inadequate sign posting, poor policing and the overall lack of a road safety culture combine to make driving in many Third World countries a harrowing experience

World of motoring
Offences in Pune, India, include 'blaring horn', 'rash driving', and 'carrying passengers on bonnet'

Fuel is often cheap in the Third World, but it may be of poor quality

Driving in the Third World

As the poorer parts of the globe develop economically they are experiencing a massive surge in motor vehicle ownership. Sadly, this is rarely accompanied by a strong road safety culture, and the result is carnage on the roads. Accident rates in some regions are soaring far higher than the West has ever experienced.

Regionally, the worst affected area is the Asia/Pacific region, which has only 16 per cent of the world's motor vehicles but 44 per cent of the world's road deaths. In Africa, some countries have more than a hundred deaths per 10,000 motor vehicles each year, compared with under two per 10,000 in the UK.

There are many reasons why developing countries have such a poor road safety record. Driving licences in many countries can be obtained with no formal training, and there is often no system of vehicle inspection equivalent to the UK's MOT test, either for private or passenger carrying vehicles.

Enforcing driving regulations is often not a high police priority, so speeding and drink-driving can be commonplace. Road safety has to fight for attention among a number of other serious problems including unemployment, poverty, crime and disease, and the political will to improve road safety is often lacking.

Emergency response to accidents is also deficient. Road accident victims have a much improved chance of survival if they receive help within the 'golden hour' immediately following an accident, but good first aid, paramedic and ambulance services are rare in developing countries.

These are all persuasive reasons to avoid driving in Third World countries. Even if you survive unscathed, you will probably find the experience so stressful that you wish you had never bothered.

If you do take the plunge, you must be continually on your guard behind the wheel. Drive defensively. That means creating as much space as you can

EXTREME CONDITIONS

around your vehicle, giving yourself a safety buffer in which you can take take avoiding action. Expect the unexpected from other drivers, such as:

- stopping without any warning in the middle of the road
- overtaking where least expected (including overtaking three abreast as you are passing a vehicle)
- swerving suddenly to avoid potholes
- passing on the nearside
- not giving way where you would expect.

Avoid driving at night, when other vehicles are likely to have faulty lights or drivers refuse to switch them on in the belief that it saves fuel. At night there's also the danger of animals roaming on the roads. In arid regions, keep off the road during wet weather. Local drivers will be unused to coping with the resulting lack of grip and their tyres are likely to be bald anyway. And in Muslim countries, avoid driving both during and immediately after Ramadan. During, because local drivers are obliged to fast during daylight hours, which does nothing for their concentration or good humour; and afterwards, because there is a lot of impatient holiday traffic on the roads and accident rates soar.

World of motoring
"Driving in Kuwait is total anarchy. I was sitting at a red traffic light when a car pulled out from the back of the queue, jumped the red light, did a handbrake turn and sped off – in full view of a police car. The urban speed limit there is 60km/h, but speeds of up to 140km/h are common."
Richard Hodge

Drivers in Third World countries face unusual hazards – such as the sacred cows which freely roam the streets of India

IN AN
EMERGENCY

Most drivers make their trip abroad without encountering any problems. But it's always wise to be prepared for the worst. Away from home you do run a greater risk of having an accident on an unfamiliar road, attracting the attention of thieves, or breaking down during a long distance drive.

Sorting out these problems can be time-consuming in a country where you are unfamiliar both with the language and ways of local bureaucracy. It pays to take extra care to avoid getting into difficulty in the first place, and to be aware of what steps you need to take to sort out trouble smoothly and calmly if it does arise.

127

Running into trouble abroad can be both expensive and time-consuming, so it pays to prepare yourself for all eventualities

Always keep your luggage stowed securely out of sight in a locked boot. If valuables are not kept secure your insurance company may not pay out if they get stolen

Motor theft

When you take your car abroad your foreign numberplate immediately marks you out as a tourist. Opportunist thieves know that you're likely to be carrying a rich haul of currency, credit cards, passports, cameras and personal possessions.

Even in a hire car you may be just as conspicuous. Some rental companies have the less than subtle habit of adorning their cars with advertising stickers. In France, hire companies all tend to register their cars in the same district, so if thieves see a car numberplate with 51 on it they can guess they're probably looking at a hire car.

Modern security systems such as alarms and immobilisers have significantly reduced the likelihood of having a car stolen, but they have done little to deter casual break-ins through a smashed window. Cars are particularly at risk when parked on the street overnight, so if possible, find a secure car park instead. Expensive alloy wheels are a tempting target for thieves, so invest in a set of locking wheel nuts.

Even when you are inside your car you may not be safe from theft. In Southern European cities thieves think nothing of snatching unguarded possessions from cars stopped at traffic lights. Be on guard for scooter riders who reach in to grab bags through an open window.

In Spain and Italy tourists are warned about thieves who pull alongside their car on the motorway, gesticulate that there is a fault with it, then rob them when they pull to the side of the road to investigate.

A few years ago there was a spate of incidents in Florida involving thieves deliberately colliding with hire cars then robbing the occupants at gun point when they stopped to inspect the damage.

It pays to keep such stories in perspective, as a few isolated incidents sometimes receive a great deal of publicity, and most people who drive abroad do so without encountering trouble. But if you are concerned about possible dangers where you are heading, it can be useful to consult the warnings for British travellers that are regularly issued and updated by the Foreign Office. You can find these on the internet, at: www.fco.gov.uk/travel.

Motorbikes are particularly vulnerable to theft, so chain your machine securely to an immovable object whenever you leave it

How to avoid car crime

◆ Don't advertise the fact that you are a tourist. Never leave maps or guide books on display inside your car

◆ Keep doors locked, windows closed and valuables hidden while driving in built-up areas

◆ Where possible park off the street in a secure, preferably attended, car park

◆ Take everything of value out of the car when leaving it. Never leave jackets or bags visible in a parked car, even if they contain nothing of value

◆ If your radio has a removable panel, take this with you when leaving the car

◆ Always lock your car, even if leaving it for just a minute, such as when paying at a filling station

◆ If another driver indicates that you should pull over, continue driving with caution until you reach a safe, busy area before stopping

◆ If another car collides with you in a secluded spot for no apparent reason, be suspicious. Carry on driving to somewhere you feel safe to stop before pulling over

◆ Avoid driving through rough or run-down urban areas, particularly in the larger American cities

◆ If you do get into a carjacking situation, on no account put up any resistance. Let the assailant get into your car and move quietly away from it

◆ If you suffer a break-in, carry out a thorough inventory to establish what has been taken and report this to the police as soon as possible. Obtain a written report from them for insurance purposes.

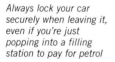

Always lock your car securely when leaving it, even if you're just popping into a filling station to pay for petrol

Most motorways abroad are provided with emergency telephones you can use to call for help if you break down. But if heading to more remote areas, consider taking a mobile phone as well

Breakdowns

The most important thing to do if your car breaks down is to alert other road users. Put on your hazard warning lights and place a warning triangle at least 50 metres behind your car on the same side of the road. On the motorway, increase this distance to 150 metres. In Spain and Turkey, you need to carry a second triangle which you should place 30 metres in front of your car.

If you have stopped on a motorway hard shoulder, remember this is a dangerous place to linger. In most circumstances it is better to climb on to the verge to wait for help rather than stay in the car. Emergency telephones are provided along most motorways abroad as in the UK, so walk to the nearest one and call for help. On freeways in the US there may be no telephones, in which case you should wait for a passing police patrol car. Raising your bonnet will alert other drivers to your predicament and someone may call the police on your behalf.

In a growing number of countries you must by law carry a reflective jacket and wear it if you have to get out of your car following an accident or breakdown (any passengers who exit the car will need their own jacket too).

Road accidents

Your first priority if you are involved in a crash is to protect the site from further accidents. Place warning triangles on the road, and stand at least 100 metres back from the scene of the accident to warn oncoming traffic. Make sure you are clearly visible to other drivers, especially at night. Stand under a street lamp or in the headlights of a car, or use a torch to draw attention to yourself.

If anybody is hurt (or in some countries, if significant damage has been caused) then you must by law call the police. There is no international standard emergency dialling code, although 112 is commonly used in Europe and 911 throughout North America.

It is a good policy to call the police even if no one is injured and the damage appears to be minor. Do not leave the scene before the police arrive, and try to avoid moving the vehicles (in Turkey it is illegal to do this). If you need to move a vehicle that is impeding traffic flow, take photographs of it from several angles before doing so. Try to make sure that witnesses do not leave before they can be interviewed by the police. Insurance companies like drivers to leave the assessment of blame to them, so don't make any admission of guilt at the scene.

If you are involved in an accident always tell your insurer or your insurer's representative in the country.

If you have a European Accident Statement, complete it at the scene. Make sure you note down the full details of the circumstances surrounding the accident, and back this up with photographs taken at the scene if possible. Note the other party's name, address, registration number and insurance company.

If you are injured, consult a local doctor and get written details of your injuries and treatment given. If you wait until you get home before seeking treatment you may find it more difficult to pursue a personal injury claim.

If you are involved in a accident in an EU country

World of motoring
"When an accident occurs on a German autobahn where there is no hard shoulder, queuing vehicles are expected to pull over to the left and right of their lanes to leave access down the middle for emergency vehicles to get to the scene."
Harry Wilby

where the other driver is liable you can now claim damages in a British court, using a solicitor in the UK – a much easier process than trying to make a claim in a foreign jurisdiction.

Helping casualties

Many countries require you to carry a first aid kit and it would be a good idea also to take some training in giving first aid to road accident casualties. The most important point is to avoid moving casualties unless there is an urgent need to do so, for instance to administer resuscitation. If a motorcyclist is breathing and in no danger of choking, do not attempt to remove his or her helmet as doing so may aggravate a neck injury. If you have to remove the helmet to resuscitate, ask someone to help by gently supporting the motorcyclist's head and neck while you do so.

Fighting fire

Many countries require you by law to carry a fire extinguisher. The most common blaze you are likely to encounter is an underbonnet fire. Never open the bonnet wide as the inrush of air can feed the flames with catastrophic results. Instead, open the bonnet a fraction and direct the extinguisher through the narrow gap.

World of motoring

"Just outside the complex where we stay in Bali there was a head-on shunt between a heavily-loaded truck and a people carrier. The truck ended up on the footway. After a few minutes the footway collapsed, exposing a deep and foul-smelling drain! After the accident local Balinese came out to put a tray of flowers and food beside the damaged vehicles, apparently to ward off ghosts."
Tim Dishman

Try not to move serious road accident casualties before the emergency services arrive or you risk aggravating their injuries

DRIVING IN
WESTERN
EUROPE

Britain may be becoming a more closely integrated part of Europe, but drivers disembarking from the ferry or Eurotunnel still experience some striking contrasts. Speed limits vary from country to country, there are unusual road signs and markings to cope with and, of course, all of mainland Europe drives on the right.

Nor can you simply hop across the channel without any preparation. You'll need to ensure that your paperwork is in order and that your insurance policy gives you fully comprehensive cover outside the UK.
  You'll need some accessories too. Each country demands by law that certain equipment is carried in the car. And don't forget to fix a GB sticker to the back of your car, and convert your headlamps so you don't dazzle oncoming traffic while driving on the right.

Despite ever-increasing EU harmonisation, driving in mainland Europe is still a very different experience to driving on British roads

FRANCE

Since the arrival of Le Shuttle it's now easier than ever to sample the delights of our nearest continental neighbour

France is by far the most popular destination for British motorists. Not only is it our closest and most convenient neighbour, it also has a vast range of natural and cultural attractions. Within a day's drive from Calais, visitors can be wine tasting in Bordeaux, exploring the coast of Brittany, skiing in the French Alps or lazing on the beach in Nice.

The relaxation of customs restrictions has given an added incentive to cross the channel. Some people head no further than the nearest hypermarket where they can pick up cheap wine and cigarettes. But even a day trip can be combined with a taste of French culture by visiting nearby attractions such as the seaside resort of Le Touquet or picturesque old town of Montreuil.

Motorists heading from crowded south east England will discover that French roads are lightly trafficked and enjoyable to use. There's a comprehensive and well-maintained network of *autoroutes* (motorways) which have a 130km/h (80mph) maximum speed limit allowing swift progress to be made.

Most are toll roads, which can add considerably to

your motoring expenses. Budget for an extra €70 in toll fees if you're heading for the south coast. Compared with British motorways, the autoroute network is well organised to ease the task of long distance driving. Every 10km or so there are rest areas (called *aires de repos*) which are ideal for a short break to stretch your legs, take a nap or have a picnic.

Service stations with a full range of facilities including restaurants come up at intervals of 30 or 40km. These tend to have a more interesting regional flavour than their counterparts in the UK, and during the holiday season they often stage entertainment, which can be a boon for bored children. Details of these can be found in english on the useful website www.autoroutes.fr.

There are also several chains of cheap, basic hotels, such as *Formule 1*, which are situated just off the autoroute and are ideal for an overnight break when heading south.

Although French autoroutes usually provide an uncongested and unstressful journey, this can change dramatically at peak holiday times when the roads from Paris fill with families leaving the city. Long traffic jams are common on the autoroutes heading south, particularly on Bastille Day (July 14) and the first weekend in August.

If your route takes you via Paris, it's a good idea to time your ferry crossing so you don't hit the *Périphérique* (the French equivalent of the M25) at rush hour when congestion can cause long delays.

If you have the time, leave the autoroutes behind and take the *Bison Futé* (crafty bison) or *Bis* routes. These follow more picturesque *Routes Nationales* (equivalent to our A-roads) but outside of towns it's still easy to make good progress along the straight tree-lined avenues of rural France. A handy free map of *Bis* routes can be obtained from tourist offices and some service stations. There's also a website *www.bison-fute.equipement.gouv.fr* which gives details of roadworks and anticipated traffic jams.

 Priority road

 Priority road ends

 Give way

 Restriction continues

 Traffic already on roundabout has right of way

 Stop at toll booth

FRANCE

French defence
"In my experience the French driver is no worse than the average British driver. Could the higher accident rate in France be contributed to by all the foreigners hurtling through to sunnier climes? Particularly the British, on the wrong side of the road!"
Wendy Furey

Local drivers

French drivers have a reputation for being intimidatingly fast, but this really applies only to the big cities. Once you've witnessed the rush hour in Paris you'll realise why you're better off sticking to the *Metro* (underground railway) while in the capital. Driving standards get noticeably more aggressive in holiday regions during August, when Parisians take their bad habits on vacation with them.

French drivers tend to treat their cars as utilitarian objects and minor scrapes and bumps are common.

Essential equipment

Like most other European countries, France insists that drivers must be at least 18 years of age. Although a British drivers are quite legal at 17 in the UK they would be committing a serious offence by driving in France: penalties include a €1500 fine and impounding the vehicle.

To be legal in France you need to equip your car with a warning triangle, a reflective jacket, a set of spare light bulbs, and fit a GB sticker (unless your car is already fitted with europlates).

Give way to the right

The motoring law most likely to catch out British drivers in France is *priorité à droite* (give way to the right). Unless there are signs to the contrary cars entering from the right have right of way, even if they are joining a main road from a side street. This means caution is needed at unmarked junctions in towns. It also applies at roundabouts unless signs specifically state otherwise (see p42). The *priorité à droite* rule is overridden on main roads marked with the *passage protégé* sign, a yellow diamond.

Speed limits

Speed limits in towns and villages start with the place name sign and end with the place name sign crossed out – don't expect to be given any other warning.

Take care when it starts to rain as lower speed limits then apply (see *Fact File*). You are also subject

The straight, tree-lined avenues of France allow easy, traffic-free touring

to lower speed limits if you have held your driving licence for less than two years. A speed limit of 50km/h applies on the autoroute in foggy conditions.

French police have started to crack down on speeding motorists. Drivers caught exceeding the speed limit by 40km/h face having their driving licence confiscated (which can make getting your car back to England awkward if you are driving alone). It is illegal to have a radar detector in your car: this is a serious offence and can result in confiscation of both the device and your vehicle.

French police are empowered to collect on-the-spot fines. More serious offences can result in your driving licence or vehicle being confiscated.

For several years now the drink-drive limit in France has been lower than in the UK, at 50mg alcohol per 100ml blood (compared with 80mg in the UK).

Sois cool man

A pop song, *Roule Cool*, has been playing on French radio and TV stations in a bid to reduce the number of young people killed and injured on the roads. Its chorus runs:
*Sois cool man
Cool
Sur les routes on roule
Cool
Sois cool man, cool man yeh
Souris
Et don't forget: courtoisie*

FRANCE

Popular vote
Take extra care when driving in France when elections are due. Traditionally there's an amnesty for all but the most serious traffic offences when a new president is elected, and speeding and parking offences soar at this time

Easily accessible from the UK, Normandy makes an ideal venue for a relaxed touring holiday

Shopping trips
If you are visiting France on a shopping trip, consult the recommended customs allowances on p65. Take care not to buy more than you can safely carry, as police on both sides of the Channel will take action if they see a dangerously overloaded car.

Parking restrictions
Parking restrictions are indicated by signs and yellow markings on the kerb. Dotted road markings indicate parking spaces; at those marked 'payant' you need to pay for parking. Spaces outlined in yellow are reserved for utility vehicles or card holders. Where there are dotted yellow lines on the edge of the pavement you may stop briefly for dropping off passengers only. Parking meters are common in towns, as are blue zones where you need to purchase and display a parking disc. In Paris, do not park or stop on red routes and do not leave a car parked in the same place for more than 24 hours.
   Look out for streets on which parking is allowed on one side for the first half of the month only, after which parking switches to the other side. This is indicated by a parking sign showing 1-15 or 16-31. *Parking souterrain* means an underground car park, sometimes more expensive but usually more secure.

Car crime
Thieves may target cars with foreign numberplates. Keep valuables out of sight and, particularly in the Marseille to Menton area, keep your car doors locked when driving to deter bag snatchers. There have been cases of muggings taking place at more isolated motorway rest areas.

Monaco and Andorra
To the south of France are two principalities – tiny Monaco on the Côte d'Azur, and rugged Andorra in the Pyrenees. Road regulations are broadly similar to those in France, although parking restrictions are tight, particularly in Monaco where caravans are not allowed.

FACT FILE FRANCE

Speed limits	Urban	Open road	Motorway
Car	50km/h	90km/h	110-130km/h
Wet weather	50km/h	80km/h	100-110km/h
Towing (up to 3.5 tonnes)	50km/h	90km/h	110-130km/h
Traffic regulations			
Essential equipment	Warning triangle, reflective jacket, spare light bulbs		
Minimum driving age	18yrs		
Drink-drive limit	50mg alcohol per 100ml blood		
Child in front seat	Minimum 10yrs (except babies up to 9 months in a rear-facing child seat)		
Seat belts	Compulsory in front and rear seats		
Motorcyclists	Must wear a crash helmet and use headlamp at all times		
Emergency telephone numbers			
Police	17		
Fire	18		
Ambulance	15		
Useful phrases			
Allumez vos lanternes	Switch on headlights		
Attention travaux	Roadworks ahead		
Chaussée déformée	Poor road surface		
Déviation	Diversion		
Gravillons	Loose chippings		
Parking payant	Charge for parking		
Péage	Road toll		
Ralentissez	Slow down		
Rappel	Restriction (such as speed limit) continues		
Route barrée	Road closed		
Stationnement interdit	No parking		

LUXEMBOURG

All that many British drivers see of Luxembourg is the autoroute (toll-free) as they speed through on their way to Germany. But the Grand Duchy of Luxembourg merits a stop in its own right, particularly to explore the part of the Ardennes that lies within its borders.

Fuel

Fuel is relatively cheap in Luxembourg, and queues can form at filling stations as drivers from surrounding countries take advantage of this. Carrying spare fuel in cans is not permitted.

Traffic signs are posted in both French and German. Police are authorised to impose on-the-spot fines. Drivers are required to flash their headlights before overtaking at night outside built-up areas. Blue zone parking systems are in operation in the main centres. Parking meters are also used in Luxembourg City.

Most British drivers head straight past Luxembourg, but it's worth pausing to explore the Grand Duchy

FACT FILE LUXEMBOURG

Speed limits	Urban	Open road	Motorway
Car	50km/h	90km/h	120km/h
Towing	50km/h	75km/h	90km/h
(motorists who have held a driving licence for less than one year must not exceed 75kph)			
Traffic regulations			
Essential equipment	Warning triangle, reflective jacket		
Minimum driving age	17yrs		
Drink-drive limit	80mg alcohol per 100ml blood		
Child in front seat	Minimum 12yrs/1.5m unless using a child restraint		
Seat belts	Compulsory in front and rear seats		
Motorcyclists	Must wear a crash helmet and use headlamp at all times		
Emergency telephone numbers			
Police	113		
Fire	112		
Ambulance	112		
Useful phrases			
See France and Germany			

NETHERLANDS

 Home zone

 Cycle path

 Parking blue zone

 Park and ride

 Compulsory route for hazardous goods

 Maximum speed limit

 No entry for motorcycles

The flat, windmill-punctuated landscape of the Netherlands makes ideal cycling territory. In a country where the 15 million inhabitants own 12 million bicycles, drivers are expected to treat cyclists with courtesy. There is a plentiful network of cycle lanes, while in home zones pedestrians and cyclists coming from the right have priority, and you should drive at a walking pace (10km/h). Traffic density in the Netherlands is the highest in Europe, so expect to encounter congestion in towns.

Give way to the right

As in most of Europe, give way to the right unless you are on a priority road indicated by a yellow diamond. You must give way to buses pulling away from bus stops in built-up areas. Trams always take priority. You should normally overtake them on the right, but only with caution and without inconveniencing passengers getting on or off the tram. If there is insufficient room to pass on the right then you may overtake, with caution, on the left.

Parking

Blue zone parking systems operate in most towns, with free parking discs available from police stations. If parking more than 30 metres from a street lamp at night you must show parking lights. And be careful when parking on main roads in Amsterdam: many allow metered parking for most of the day but cars still there when the rush hour starts will be towed. Check signs for the precise times as recovering a car costs over £100. Do not park on roads marked *Stop-verbod*, and do not park against the direction of traffic flow. As in most European countries, it is illegal to use a mobile phone while driving. Police are authorised to impose on-the-spot fines.

FACT FILE NETHERLANDS

Speed limits	Urban	Open road	Motorway
Car	50km/h	80-100km/h	120km/h
Towing	50km/h	80km/h	80km/h
Traffic regulations			
Essential equipment	Warning triangle		
Minimum driving age	18yrs		
Drink-drive limit	50mg alcohol per 100ml blood		
Child in front seat	Minimum 12yrs/1.5m unless using a child restraint		
Seat belts	Compulsory in front and rear seats		
Motorcyclists	Must wear a crash helmet		
Emergency telephone numbers			
Police	112		
Fire	112		
Ambulance	112		
Useful phrases			
Doorgaand verkeer gestremd	No throughway		
Langzaam rijden	Slow down		
Opspattend grind	Loose chippings		
Pas op!	Attention		
Rechtsaf toegestaan	Right turn allowed		
Stop-verbod	No parking		
Tegenliggers	Traffic from opposite direction		
Wegomlegging	Detour		
Werk in uitvoering	Work in progress		

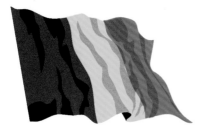

BELGIUM

 Overtake on left or right

 Give way to cyclists crossing side road

 No parking from 1st to 15th of each month

 End of home zone

 Cruise control prohibited

Belgian drivers have a poor reputation, borne out by an unusually high road casualty rate by Western European standards. One explanation for this is that Belgium was one of the last European countries to introduce a compulsory driving test. It also doesn't help that there are a large number of foreign drivers living in Brussels, who aren't all used to the strong local convention of giving way to the right: the foreign driver gives way at an intersection and is promptly rear-ended by a local driver who assumes that the car in front will assert its right of way. Always be on the alert for vehicles joining from the right without giving way, even if you are apparently on a main road. Always give way to trams.

Regulations
Blue zone parking systems operate in major towns. Look out for signs indicating that cars should park fully or partly on the pavement. Police are authorised to impose on-the-spot fines. Filling stations often close on Sundays. It is illegal to leave a dog unattended in a parked car. Do not use cruise control where signs prohibit it.

Road signs
Two languages are spoken in Belgium, Flemish and French. This can be confusing for visiting drivers because road signs in the north of the country are in Flemish, while in the south they are in French (signs in Brussels tend to be bi-lingual. Many towns have different names in each language, and it's easy to be caught out when you cross from one linguistic region to the other and signs start using the alternative spelling. Place names likely to confuse include:
Liege – Luik
Ypres – Ieper
Lille – Rijsel
Mons – Bergen
Tournai – Doornik
De Han – Le Coq
Kortrijk – Courtrai
Veurne – Furnes
Zoutleeuw – Léau.

Cutting comment
In France, one of the worst insults to hurl at another motorist is *Il conduit comme un Belge* (he drives like a Belgian)

FACT FILE BELGIUM

Speed limits	Urban	Open road	Motorway
Car	50km/h	90km/h	120km/h
Towing	50km/h	90km/h	120km/h
Traffic regulations			
Essential equipment	Warning triangle, reflective jacket		
Minimum driving age	18yrs		
Drink-drive limit	50mg alcohol per 100ml blood		
Child in front seat	Minimum 12yrs unless using a child restraint		
Seat belts	Compulsory in front and rear seats		
Motorcyclists	Must wear a crash helmet and use headlamp at all times		
Emergency telephone numbers			
Police	101		
Fire	100		
Ambulance	100		
Useful phrases			
See France and Netherlands			

Such tranquil scenes aren't necessarily the rule in Belgium, which has a poor record for road safety

GERMANY

Lower speed limit applies in the wet

Expressway

One way street

Keep distance shown

Bus or tram stop

German drivers have a reputation for being fast but disciplined. Roads are smooth and impeccably maintained.

Motorways

Germany has a dense network of *Autobahnen* (motorways) famous for being free of speed restrictions. However, this only applies to parts of the network. Where speed limits are posted they are generally obeyed and in any case rigorously enforced.

Even on derestricted stretches traffic congestion often keeps speeds down. A 100-mile jam was once recorded on the A7 from Hamburg to the Danish border. Routes to the Alps can be particularly busy at weekends in the ski season and summer holiday time. Don't run out of fuel on the Autobahn: it's an offence. Police are empowered to impose on-the-spot fines.

Free right turn

One traffic rule that Germany inherited from the former East Germany is a free right turn at red traffic lights. Where a green arrow is signposted at the lights, you may turn right on red after stopping to check the way is clear. At night traffic lights are often switched off or flash amber, in which case obey the give way or stop sign posted at the traffic lights. Give way to buses pulling out.

In heavily congested traffic German drivers behave with typical order. At junctions and where two lanes merge into one the zipper rule (*Reissverschluss*) comes into play, with cars giving way one at a time.

To park in Germany you usually need to buy a blue parking disc (*Parkscheibe*) available from newsagents and service stations, although parking vouchers (*Parkschein*) and parking meters are also common.

In some city centres entry for cars is restricted depending on their emissions. These areas are indicated by signs showing green, yellow or red vignettes. To enter you must display a vignette, which is available from approved garages on production of your car registration document and a small fee.

FACT FILE GERMANY

Speed limits	Urban	Open road	Motorway
Car	50km/h	100km/h	130km/h *(recommended)*
Towing	50km/h	80km/h	80km/h
Traffic regulations			
Essential equipment	Warning triangle		
Minimum driving age	17yrs		
Drink-drive limit	50mg alcohol per 100ml blood		
Child in front seat	Minimum 12yrs/1.5m unless using a child restraint		
Seat belts	Compulsory in front and rear seats		
Motorcyclists	Must wear a crash helmet and use headlamp at all times		
Emergency telephone numbers			
Police	112		
Fire	112		
Ambulance	112		
Useful phrases			
Achtung	Attention		
Ausfahrt	Exit		
Bei Nässe	In wet weather		
Gefahr	Danger		
Licht einschalten	Turn on headlamps		
Ölspur	Oil on road		
Parkplatz	Parking lot		
Rasthof	Service area		
Rollsplitt	Loose chippings		
Schlechte wegstrecke	Uneven road		
Stau	Traffic congestion		
Tankstelle	Filling station		
Vorfahrt	Right of way		

AUSTRIA

 Diversion

 Buses only

 Street lights not lit all night long

 Tram may turn on red or amber

Austria's alpine roads give some spectacular touring but be careful when setting out between November and May as higher passes can be blocked by snow. Snow chains are compulsory in mountainous areas in winter.

Mountain roads
Give way to buses on mountain roads. When meeting other traffic the vehicle that can give way most easily should stop, so be ready to give way whether you are going up or down.

Vignette
To use Austria's motorway network you must purchase a vignette and display it on your windscreen. Vignettes are available for one year, two months or ten days, and they are available at border crossings and service stations. At the time of writing costs were:
Ten days: €7.70 (car); €4.30 (motorbike)
Two months: €22.20 (car); €10.90 (motorbike)
One year: €73.80 (car); €29.00 (motorbike)
A vignette also allows you 15 per cent discount on some tunnel toll fees.

Parking
At short-term parking zones (*Kurzparkzone*) you need to purchase a ticket from local shops and fill in your time of arrival. When parking at night you must leave you sidelights on unless street lighting is provided. But look out for red-banded lamp posts – these are extinguished at midnight, whereupon your car might get a ticket if it isn't lit.

Traffic
Traffic is generally not heavy but expect some delays if you're heading across the border towards Hungary, Slovakia or the Czech Republic. Restrictions on car use can be imposed at times when air pollution reaches high levels.

FACT FILE AUSTRIA

Speed limits	Urban	Open road	Motorway
Car	50km/h	100km/h	130km/h*
Towing	50km/h	80km/h	100km/h
	110km/h limit applies on some motorways at night		
Traffic regulations			
Essential equipment	Warning triangle, first aid kit, reflective jacket		
Minimum driving age	18yrs		
Drink-drive limit	50mg alcohol per 100ml blood		
Child in front seat	Minimum 12yrs/1.5m unless using a child restraint		
Seat belts	Compulsory in front and rear seats		
Motorcyclists	Must wear a crash helmet and use headlamp at all times		
Emergency telephone numbers			
Police	112		
Fire	112		
Ambulance	112		
Useful phrases			
Hupverbot	No horn use allowed		
Glatteisgefahr	Icy road		
Lawinen Gefahr	Danger of avalanche		
Steinschlag	Falling rocks		
Verengte Fahrbahn	Road narrows		

SWITZERLAND

Tunnel (lights compulsory)

Level crossing

Single-carriageway motorway

Blue zone parking

Slow lane

While in Switzerland drivers may want to consider leaving behind the car and taking to public transport instead. Switzerland has an impressive network of trains, buses and trams, supplemented in the mountains by numerous cable cars, mountain railways and chairlifts.

Winter driving

As in Austria, care is needed when driving on alpine roads during the winter months. The rule of the road here is to give way to vehicles ascending, and you must also give way to postal vehicles. Beware of some roads which change their direction of traffic flow depending on the time of day. Border crossings and tunnels in the mountains can be congested. It's compulsory to switch off your engine while waiting in stationary traffic.

Vignette

A vignette is needed to use the motorways but unlike Austria only one type is available and this covers a whole year (or to be precise, the 14 months from December 1 to January 31). Vignettes are available at border crossings, service stations and post offices, or in advance from the Switzerland Travel Centre at 10 Wardour Street, London W1D 6QF. The cost of the vignette is currently £21. If you are towing a trailer or caravan you have to purchase two vignettes.

Traffic rules

Give way to the right except on main roads marked with a yellow diamond. Dipped headlamps are compulsory in tunnels. Road signs may be given in French, German or Italian. Buses pulling out have priority. Blue zones operate where you must display a disc to park. Parking meters are also common. Parking on the pavement is not permitted. The police are authorised to impose on-the-spot fines. If you need to wear spectacles to drive you must carry a spare pair in the car.

FACT FILE SWITZERLAND

Speed limits	Urban	Open road	Motorway
Car	50km/h	80-100km/h	120km/h
Towing	50km/h	80km/h*	80km/h
	*60km/h if laden weight exceeds 1000kg		
Traffic regulations			
Essential equipment	Warning triangle		
Minimum driving age	18yrs		
Drink-drive limit	80mg alcohol per 100ml blood		
Child in front seat	Minimum 7yrs unless using a child restraint		
Seat belts	Compulsory in front and rear seats		
Motorcyclists	Must wear a crash helmet and use headlamp at all times		
Emergency telephone numbers			
Police	117		
Fire	118		
Ambulance	144		
Useful phrases			
See France, Germany and Italy			

Switzerland offers some of the most spectacular driving in Europe, but care is needed on its mountain roads, especially in winter

IRELAND

Straight
ahead only

Parking
permitted

Roundabout

Give way

Dip in road
ahead

Unguarded
level
crossing

Road
narrows

Driving in the Republic of Ireland poses few problems for motorists from the UK. Traffic drives on the left and generally moves at a relaxed pace, although drivers can occasionally be unpredictable (many older motorists have never taken a formal driving test) and accident rates are higher than in the UK.

Ireland has embarked on a large-scale road improvement programme which is making driving there much quicker and easier. One difference from the UK is that distances are indicated in kilometres on the new green sign posts, although some older signs still show miles. Speed limits are in km/h. Most signs are in English, although you may see the Gaelic 'give way' sign, *Géill Slí*, and many place names are in Gaelic.

Passing lanes

Main highways have passing lanes, separated from the main carriageway by a broken yellow line. You are expected to use this to move over and let faster vehicles pass, but take care as the hard shoulder is frequently potholed. Minor roads can also be in a poor state of repair, and look out for livestock wandering on to the road in rural areas.

Insurance

As when heading to other European countries you will need to take your vehicle registration document (or a letter of authority for a company or hire car) and arrange fully comprehensive insurance before setting out. Note that your vehicle may not be driven by Irish residents during your visit, except by a garage employee with your written permission.

Parking

Parking is controlled by single and double yellow lines as it is in the UK. Cars parked illegally may be towed away.

Car rental

Hire cars tend to be expensive in Ireland. Check with your rental company if you intend driving across the border from Northern Ireland.

FACT FILE IRELAND

Speed limits	Urban	Open road	Motorway
Car	50km/h	100km/h	120km/h
Towing	50km/h	80km/h	80km/h
Traffic regulations			
Essential equipment	None		
Minimum driving age	17yrs		
Drink-drive limit	80mg alcohol per 100ml blood		
Child in front seat	No age restriction but must use seatbelt or child restraint		
Seat belts	Compulsory in front and rear seats		
Motorcyclists	Must wear a crash helmet		
Emergency telephone numbers			
Police	999 / 112		
Fire	999 / 112		
Ambulance	999 / 112		

Glorious scenery and a relaxed pace of life make Ireland the perfect setting for a touring holiday

DRIVING IN
SCANDINAVIA

Scandinavia offers superb touring opportunities, with picturesque forests, dramatic fjords, soaring mountains and an abundance of crystal clear fresh air. In midsummer Scandinavia's far north offers the added attraction of 24-hour daylight. Conversely, in winter drivers must prepare for dark days and icy roads on which snow chains or studded tyres are a necessity.

As you might expect from the home of Volvo, Scandinavia has a strong road safety culture. Speed limits are low and backed by hefty fines, drink-driving regulations are strict, and vehicles must use dipped lights at all times to ensure maximum visibility. Because of this, countries like Sweden and Norway have road safety records similar to the UK.

That's not to say that roads don't have their special hazards, particularly the elk and reindeer that lurk in the forest ready to run out in front of unsuspecting motorists. Be particularly careful when driving at dusk or dawn.

Scandinavians tend to be polite, cautious drivers, although in winter the aplomb with which they tackle ice-packed roads in cars equipped with studded tyres has to be seen to be believed.

Scandinavia boasts some dramatic landscapes – and its roads are among the safest in the world too

DENMARK

Traffic merges

Minimum speed limit

Advisory speed limit

Place of interest

1 hour parking zone

Denmark's fine network of uncrowded secondary roads makes it a good venue for a relaxed touring holiday. Look out for the scenic Marguerite Route which takes in some of the finest sights. It's marked by signs showing a white daisy on a brown background. Motorways are toll-free. Cycling is popular in Denmark, so take care in built-up areas and always check for approaching cyclists before crossing a cycle lane.

Ferries
Ferries can fill up at peak periods, so it pays to book them in advance. A timetable is available from FDM, the Danish motoring club which has offices in major towns. Denmark is now linked to Sweden by the 16km Øresund bridge. A toll is payable, as it is on the Great Belt Connection between Zealand and Funen.

Daytime lights
A line of white triangles on the road means give way. Be prepared to give way to bicycles, and also to buses signalling to pull out. Use dipped headlamps day and night.

Parking
Parking is permitted on the right (in the direction of traffic) only, and you may park with two wheels on the pavement as long as pedestrians are not inconvenienced. Use a parking disc where limited waiting times are shown, setting the clock on the disc to your time of arrival. An on-the-spot fine can be levied on transgressors. In Copenhagen parking is permitted in marked areas only.

FACT FILE DENMARK

Speed limits	Urban	Open road	Motorway
Car	50km/h	80km/h	110km/h
Towing	50km/h	70km/h	70km/h
Traffic regulations			
Essential equipment	Warning triangle		
Minimum driving age	17yrs		
Drink-drive limit	50mg alcohol per 100ml blood		
Child in front seat	Minimum 3yrs unless using a child restraint		
Seat belts	Compulsory in front and rear seats		
Motorcyclists	Must wear a crash helmet and use headlamp at all times		
Emergency telephone numbers			
Police	112		
Fire	112		
Ambulance	112		
Useful phrases			
Fare	Danger		
Fodgængerovergang	Pedestrian crossing		
Gennemkørsel forbudt	No through road		
Indkørsel forbudt	No entry		
Korsvej	Crossroads		
Omkørsel	Diversion		
Parkering forbudt	No parking		
Vejen er spærret	Road closed		

SWEDEN

Wide horizons

"Many people do not realise that Sweden is a very large country, actually three times the size of the British Isles. If you drove from north to south at a normal pace with stops and night breaks, it would take you the best part of a week"
Birgitta Morris

Beware elk

Flervägs–stopp

Stop

Tunnel

Slow lane

Sweden's motorways are confined to the south of the country around Stockholm. They are toll-free. More characteristic of the country are the miles of picturesque, lightly trafficked country roads. Many have wide shoulders which it is usual to pull onto in order to let following vehicles overtake. Speed limits are strictly enforced – exceed the limit by more than 30km/h and you risk having your licence confiscated. The drink-drive limit is much lower than in most countries at 20mg alcohol per 100ml blood. Swedish police are authorised to impose fines for minor traffic offences on the spot but not to collect them (the fines are paid at a post office).

Winter driving

Winters are severe in Sweden. Roads can be closed during the winter months, and studded tyres are permitted between November 1st and the first Monday after Easter. In spring beware of damage to road surfaces caused by frost.

Traffic rules

Dipped headlamps are compulsory day and night. Overtaking on the right as well as the left is permitted on multi-lane highways with a speed limit of 70km/h or less. Merge in turn where two lanes become one. Filling stations are few and far between in the north. Not all sell diesel, and LPG is rare.

Elk and reindeer

Half of Sweden is forested, and in these areas special care is needed due to elk and reindeer wandering on to the road. Report any collision involving one to the police.

Parking

Take care when leaving your car in Stockholm overnight. Each street is swept on one night each week, and if your car is left in a street on a cleaning night you will be fined. Foreign vehicles do not have to pay congestion charges in Stockholm.

DRIVING IN **SCANDINAVIA**

FACT FILE SWEDEN

Speed limits	Urban	Open road	Motorway
Car	50km/h	70-90km/h	110km/h
Towing	50km/h	70-80km/h	80km/h
Traffic regulations			
Essential equipment	Warning triangle		
Minimum driving age	18yrs		
Drink-drive limit	20mg alcohol per 100ml blood		
Child in front seat	Minimum 7yrs unless using a child restraint		
Seat belts	Compulsory in front and rear seats		
Motorcyclists	Must wear a crash helmet and use headlamp at all times		
Emergency telephone numbers			
Police	112		
Fire	112		
Ambulance	112		
Useful phrases			
Enkelriktat	One way		
Farlig kurva	Dangerous bend		
Grusad väg	Loose chippings		
Höger	Right		
Ingen infart	No entrance		
Parkering förbjuden	No parking		
Polisstation	Police station		
Vänster	Left		
Varning för tåg	Level crossing		

NORWAY

M Passing place

Bus lane

Lane ends

Traffic joining has priority

Ski runs

Tunnel

Romantic journey

"Three weeks and 3500 miles in Scandinavia were a journey of mystery and romance. We passed beneath a waterfall on the 'Trolls Path', and descended the hairpins of the 'Eagles Road', the highest pass in Norway from which a cruise ship in the fjord below looked like a tiny toy."
Fiona Haig

Norway's dramatic fjorded and mountainous landscape is pierced by numerous road tunnels, and you will frequently encounter tolls (if not trolls, which are rarely a problem nowadays). The number of ferry crossings needed along the west coast can add considerably to journey times.

Mountain roads

Great care is needed on minor mountain roads, especially when there is a risk of snow or ice. In winter many highways are closed and the authorities concentrate on keeping a limited number of major routes free of snow. If in doubt, ask local advice before setting out and go well prepared with emergency clothing and provisions in case you run into trouble. Winter tyres are mandatory from November to April. Narrow roads have *Møteplass* or 'meeting points' at the side of the road; when the space is on your side you are obliged to stop and give way to oncoming traffic. Only experienced caravanners should tackle mountain roads, some of which are off-limits to caravans altogether.

Speed limits

Speed limits are low (even on motorways 90km/h is the maximum allowed). This can make progress slow, but exceed the limits at your peril. They are strictly enforced and fines (or even jail sentences) are severe. The police can impose on-the-spot fines. Use dipped headlights day and night.

Parking

Parking laws should be taken seriously. Yellow parking meters allow stopping for up to one hour, grey meters for two hours and brown meters three hours.

Fuel

Fill up when you get the chance in remote areas. Filling stations may not accept credit cards, and LPG is not widely available.

FACT FILE NORWAY

Speed limits	Urban	Open road	Motorway
Car	50km/h	80km/h	90km/h
Towing	50km/h	80km/h	80km/h
Traffic regulations			
Essential equipment	Warning triangle		
Minimum driving age	17yrs		
Drink-drive limit	20mg alcohol per 100ml blood		
Child in front seat	Minimum 4yrs unless using a child restraint		
Seat belts	Compulsory in front and rear seats		
Motorcyclists	Must wear a crash helmet and use headlamp at all times		
Emergency telephone numbers			
Police	112		
Fire	110		
Ambulance	113		
Useful phrases			
All stans førbudt	No stopping		
Enveiskjøring	One-way traffic		
Ikke møte	No overtaking		
Kjør sakte	Slow down		
Løs grus	Loose chippings		
Møteplass	Passing place		
Omkjøring	Diversion		
Veiarbeide	Roadworks		

FINLAND

Beware reindeer

Detour

No parking: 8am-5pm (Mon-Fri)

No parking: 8am-1pm (Sat)

No parking: 8am-2pm (Sun)

Finland has a well-maintained system of main roads including a small motorway network. There are no road tolls, and many of the numerous ferries are free of charge too.

Winter driving

Winter conditions are harsh and snow tyres are compulsory from December to the end of February. Visiting motorists can hire these locally. Care should be taken on the gravel roads, common in less populated areas, which can be in poor condition after the winter. Dipped headlamps are compulsory day and night throughout the year.

Give way to the right at intersections, and always give priority to trams and buses pulling out. Elk and reindeer crossing the road are a serious hazard and a collision with one must be reported to the police. Accidents involving another road user should be reported to the Finnish Motor Insurers' Centre (tel: 9-680-401).

Fuel availability

Most filling stations close at night and LPG is not available. Fuel can be significantly more expensive in the north and filling stations few and far between. There are parking meters in some towns and infringements are treated seriously.

Finland is a country of lakes and forests; car ferries are numerous but most are toll-free

DRIVING IN **SCANDINAVIA**

FACT FILE FINLAND

Speed limits	Urban	Open road	Motorway
Car	50km/h	80-100km/h	120km/h
Towing	50km/h	80km/h	80km/h
Traffic regulations			
Essential equipment	Warning triangle		
Minimum driving age	18yrs		
Drink-drive limit	50mg alcohol per 100ml blood		
Child in front seat	No age restriction but must use seatbelt or child restraint		
Seat belts	Compulsory in front and rear seats		
Motorcyclists	Must wear a crash helmet and use headlamp at all times		
Emergency telephone numbers			
Police	10022		
Fire	112		
Ambulance	112		
Useful phrases			
Aja hitaasti	Slow down		
Aluerajoitus	Local speed limit		
Lossi-farja	Ferry		
Kelirikko	Road damaged by frost		
Kunnossapitotyo	Roadworks		
Moottoritie	Motorway		

DRIVING IN
SOUTHERN
EUROPE

The warm climes of Southern Europe are famously associated with a hot-blooded Latin temperament. Nowhere is this more apparent than on the roads. Mediterranean drivers are fast, eager to seize the slightest chance to move their way up the traffic flow and take an unashamed sense of fun in their driving.

The downside of a driving culture which relies on speed and swift reactions is that when something does go wrong, drivers often haven't left themselves enough space to get out of trouble. Accident rates are two to three times higher in southern Europe compared with the north.

Few British motorists drive their own cars as far as southern Spain or Greece, but many of us hire cars there. Holidays may be all about relaxing, but always remember that being in charge of a motor vehicle is a serious business wherever you are. Never drop your safety standards just because you are in a carefree atmosphere away from home: don't drink and drive, always wear a seatbelt and obey traffic regulations, whatever local drivers may appear to do.

The typically narrow and crowded streets of towns in southern Europe are picturesque but pose an extra hazard for drivers

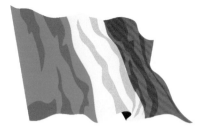

ITALY

Italy sees the point
A newly-introduced penalty points system which threatens disqualification for persistent offenders is showing signs of taming the famously lawless Italian driver. In the 50 days after penalty points were introduced, serious road accidents fell by almost a third

Parking restrictions

Snow chains required

No fires permitted

Horizontal traffic light

Stop – police

Italy's impressive motorway or *autostrada* network allows rapid progress across the country, but expect to cover much less ground once you leave the motorway. Most motorways are toll roads. Credit cards are usually accepted, or you can purchase a Viacard from service stations or tourist offices. Carry plenty of cash as Italian petrol stations do not accept credit cards, particularly in rural areas. As in France, police may monitor the average speed of motorists between motorway tolls. Radar detectors are strictly prohibited.

Car theft
Theft is a problem in Italian towns and cities, particularly Naples and Rome, where moped riders snatch bags from stationary cars at traffic lights. Keep your windows closed and doors locked in town, and never leave valuables, bags or jackets on display.

Fog
Despite Italy's hot summer climate, in the winter months fog can be a hazard on roads in the north, and in the Italian Alps it is compulsory to carry snow chains from October 15th to April 30th. It is now mandatory to use dipped headlamps at all times outside built-up areas. When two oncoming cars are both turning left at a crossroads, they must turn in front of each other, not behind as is usual in the UK. If you have an overhanging load, such as a bicycle strapped to the rear of the car, you must fit a reflective square panel to it. If carrying more than one dog in your car, you must ensure they are kept caged or separated from the driver by bars.

Fuel
LPG is available in the north of the country but less easy to find further south. Carrying spare fuel in a can is not permitted. A parking disc must be displayed in blue zones in towns, but don't even try to park close to busy historic city centres.

FACT FILE ITALY

Speed limits	Urban	Open road	Motorway
Car	50km/h	90-110km/h	130km/h
Towing	50km/h	70km/h	80km/h
Traffic regulations			
Essential equipment	Warning triangle, reflective jacket		
Minimum driving age	18yrs		
Drink-drive limit	50mg alcohol per 100ml blood		
Child in front seat	Minimum 12yrs unless using a child restraint		
Seat belts	Compulsory in front and rear seats		
Motorcyclists	Must wear a crash helmet and use headlamp at all times		
Emergency telephone numbers			
Police	112		
Fire	115		
Ambulance	118		
Useful phrases			
Destra	Right		
Incrocio	Crossroads		
Lavori in corso	Roadworks		
Nord	North		
Rallentare	Slow down		
Senso unico	One-way street		
Senso vietato	No entry		
Sinistra	Left		
Sosta vietata	No parking		
Sud	South		
Svolta	Bend or turning		
Tornante	Winding road		
Uscita	Exit		

SPAIN

Bull fight

Spain's supreme court has granted a reprieve for the giant bull silhouettes that form such an evocative feature of the Spanish landscape. The bulls – promotional hoardings for Osborne brandy – have been a source of heated debate since 1989 when roadside advertising was outlawed in Spain

Restricted parking zone

No parking on Monday, Wednesday, Friday or Sunday

No parking on Tuesday, Thursday or Saturday

Use dipped headlamps

Water

Leave the crowded coastal strip behind and Spain is a wonderful country to explore by car. Roads are generally well-maintained and free of traffic, and Spain has a fine *autopista* (motorway) network, much of which is toll-free. A bail bond is no longer required when taking your car to Spain.

Turning left

When turning left across oncoming traffic it is usually necessary first to pull off the right of the road and stop before crossing both carriageways once the road is clear. Do not turn left across an unbroken white line down the centre of the road; drive on until you reach a turning place. Give way to the right where no priority is signposted. It is compulsory to carry a spare pair of glasses if you need to wear them to drive.

Weather conditions

Inland Spain has a continental climate, fiercely hot in summer when air conditioning can be a boon. Winter can be surprisingly cold (don't forget Madrid is half a mile above sea level) so watch out for ice on the roads and snow in hillier parts.

Breakdowns

Cars in Spain must by law carry two warning triangles. If you break down or are involved in an accident, place one triangle in front of and one behind the car. A reflective jacket must also be carried, to be worn in the event of a motorway breakdown. Stay alert in cities and at motorway service stations for con-men who distract the driver by indicating a defect to their car while an accomplice reaches inside and grabs their valuables.

Parking

Parking in many towns is controlled by blue zones (*zonas azul*) where a disc must be displayed. Do not park on main roads with a continuous white line along the edge. The police are authorised to impose on-the-spot fines. Only fully hands-free mobile phones (without earpiece or headphones) are permitted.

FACT FILE SPAIN

Speed limits	Urban	Open road	Motorway
Car	50km/h	90-100km/h	120km/h
Towing	50km/h	70-80km/h	80km/h
Traffic regulations			
Essential equipment	Two warning triangles, spare bulbs, reflective jacket		
Minimum driving age	18yrs		
Drink-drive limit	50mg alcohol per 100ml blood		
Child in front seat	Minimum 12yrs unless using a child restraint		
Seat belts	Compulsory in front and rear seats		
Motorcyclists	Must wear a crash helmet and use headlamp at all times		
Emergency telephone numbers			
Police	112		
Fire	112		
Ambulance	112		
Useful phrases			
Abierto	(Road) open		
Carretera de peaje	Toll road		
Ceda el paso	Give way		
Cerrado	(Road) closed		
Despacio	Slow		
Desviación	Detour		
Estación de peaje	Toll station		
Gravilla	Loose chippings		
Obras	Roadworks		
Peligro	Danger		
Prioridad	Right of way		
Prohibición	Prohibited		
Salida	Exit		

PORTUGAL

Portugal has the poorest road safety record in Europe and great care should be taken when driving there, especially on busy coastal roads; the N125 near Faro has a particularly bad reputation. Avoid driving on the first weekend in August, when roads are clogged with local holiday traffic.

Motorways

Motorways (*auto-estradas*) are the best way to cover long distances quickly and safely, although most are toll roads. Avoid the green lanes which are reserved for local drivers who subscribe to an automatic payment system. Keep your speed between 30 and 50km/h when crossing the Tagus bridge in Lisbon, and don't run out of fuel on it either – it's an offence. LPG is not available in Portugal, and spare fuel must not be carried in cans.

Give way to the right

Be prepared to give way to the right even if you appear to be on a main road. Overtake stationary trams on the right only, when passengers have finished getting on and off.

New drivers

Drivers who have held their licence for less than a year must not exceed 90km/h and must display a yellow '90' disc on the rear of their car. These are available from Portuguese Automobile Club (ACP) offices. If driving a car not registered in your own name you will need a special form or *Autorizacao*, available from motoring organisations. It is permissible to take your car to Portugal for a maximum of 180 days in any 12-month period, but you must not lend it to anyone else while you are there.

Parking

Blue zone parking operates in Lisbon, elsewhere parking meters are common. In major towns unemployed men often wave drivers to a parking space in return for a small tip. The police are authorised to impose on-the-spot fines.

Drink problem
Portugal restored its drink-drive level to 50mg of alcohol per 100ml of blood, the same as in most other European countries, after a brief trial of a 20mg limit. The lower limit was suspended after an outcry from wine producers, who complained their sales had fallen by nearly a third

FACT FILE PORTUGAL

Speed limits	Urban	Open road	Motorway
Car	50km/h	90km/h	120km/h
Towing	50km/h	70km/h	100km/h
(motorists who have held a driving licence for less than one year must not exceed 90km/h)			
Traffic regulations			
Essential equipment	Warning triangle, reflective jacket		
Minimum driving age	18yrs		
Drink-drive limit	50mg alcohol per 100ml blood		
Child in front seat	Minimum 12yrs unless using a child restraint		
Seat belts	Compulsory in front and rear seats		
Motorcyclists	Must wear a crash helmet and use headlamp at all times		
Emergency telephone numbers			
Police	112		
Fire	112		
Ambulance	112		
Useful phrases			
Fronteira	Border		
Gasóleo	Diesel		
Itinerário principal	Main road		
Limite de velocidade	Speed limit		
Portagem	Toll		
Sem chumbo	Unleaded petrol		

GREECE

Driving on mainland Greece can be a hectic experience, but the pace is rather more relaxed on the Greek islands where most holidaymakers are bound. Look out for weaving motorbikes and scooters in the resorts, as well as tourists unfamiliar with local conditions. Highways often have a white line along the nearside and slower traffic is expected to pull across it to allow overtaking.

Local traffic

Off the main highway roads can be narrow and winding with precipitous drops. Be ready to pull in for local traffic, including buses and coaches which you'll encounter on the unlikeliest roads. Horn use is frequent in Greece but bear in mind that you can be fined for using a horn without good reason.

Insurance

It may be necessary to drive on unmade roads to get to your villa or local beaches, so ensure that your hire insurance covers you on these. Check also that you are covered if you plan to take your car on an island ferry. Don't be surprised if you are required to reverse your car on to the ferry when embarking.

Fuel

In rural areas fuel stations may close at evenings and weekends, so fill up in advance. Not all accept credit cards. LPG is not available, and it is not permitted to carry spare fuel in cans.

Motorbike hire

Many tourists hire a moped or motorbike and end up regretting it after having a nasty accident. Only hire one if you are already an experienced rider. The law has anyway recently changed so that a valid driving licence with at least category A1 (light motorcycle) is required to hire even a moped. Category P, which is valid in the UK for riding mopeds up to 50cc, is not recognised in Greece. Greek law requires riders to wear a crash helmet on a scooter, moped or motorcycle.

Crossing from one Greek island to another by ferry is easy, but check that your hire car agreement covers ferry trips

FACT FILE GREECE

Speed limits	Urban	Open road	Motorway
Car	50km/h	110km/h	120km/h
Towing	50km/h	110km/h	120km/h
Motorcycle	40km/h	70km/h	90km/h
Traffic regulations			
Essential equipment	Warning triangle, first aid kit, fire extinguisher		
Minimum driving age	17yrs		
Drink-drive limit	50mg alcohol per 100ml blood		
Child in front seat	Minimum 10yrs		
Seat belts	Compulsory in front seats		
Motorcyclists	Must wear a crash helmet and obey lower speed limits		
Emergency telephone numbers			
Police	100		
Fire	199		
Ambulance	166 *(Athens)*		
Useful phrases			
Αδιεξοδος	Dead end		
Δρόμος κλειοτός	Road closed		
Κίνδυνος	Danger		
Ολο δεξιά	Keep right		
Οδικά έργα	Road works ahead		
Απότομος λόφος	Steep hill		
Στροφές	Winding road		

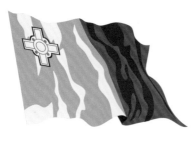

MALTA

No horn blowing

No overtaking by heavy vehicles

Tunnel warning

Hazard at edge of road

Tourist destination

Place name

Malta is a reassuringly familiar destination for British holidaymakers. Two centuries of British influence has left an enduring mark on Maltese culture, and also its driving habits. Not only does the island drive on the left, it retains plenty of familiar street furniture – including red telephone and pillar boxes – and there are a surprising number of 1960s British cars still on the road. However, the enthusiastic driving style owes more to Mediterranean than British influences (locals joke that they don't drive on the left or right, but in the shade).

Busy roads
Malta is a small island with a large number of cars and roads can get congested, particularly along the coast roads at weekends and in Valetta during rush hours. A short car ferry ride connects Malta with the neighbouring island of Gozo.

Regulations
The Maltese Highway Code looks very similar to the British one. Differences to watch out for include the speed limits (see *Fact File*) and rules on giving way on narrow roads: the driver nearest to the wider section of road must by law reverse to give way. On a hill vehicles going uphill have priority over those coming down.

In tunnels you must switch on your headlights and stay in lane. Take care when parking as Malta has introduced zones where illegally-parked cars will be wheelclamped or towed away. These zones should be clearly marked with signs.

In the event of an accident you must inform the police and not move any of the vehicles concerned until they have arrived.

Fuel stations
Filling up on a Saturday can be a good idea as many fuel stations close on Sundays and public holidays (although some have automatic pumps for use out of hours).

FACT FILE MALTA

Speed limits	Urban	Open road	Motorway
Car	50km/h	80km/h	-
Towing	50km/h	80km/h	-
Traffic regulations			
Essential equipment	Warning triangle		
Minimum driving age	18yrs		
Drink-drive limit	80mg alcohol per 100ml blood		
Child in front seat	Up to 3yrs must use restraint		
Seat belts	Compulsory in front and rear seats		
Motorcyclists	Must wear a crash helmet		
Emergency telephone numbers			
Police	191		
Fire	199		
Ambulance	196		

Reflecting its long association with Britain, in Malta vehicles drive on the left-hand side of the road

CYPRUS

Cyprus has had a long association with Britain and it is a popular destination for holidaymakers as well as having a large ex-pat community. Since 1974 Cyprus has been divided in two: the southern Republic of Cyprus is joining the EU in May 2004, while the Turkish Republic of North Cyprus is not recognised by the British Government. Recent improvements in relations between the two halves mean that it is possible for tourists to make day trips from South to North across the Atilla Line (known as the Green Line in Nicosia).

Hire cars

Cyprus drives on the left which makes life easier for British tourists who wish to hire a car. Do check the condition of your car carefully as some – especially from local outfits – are in poor condition. Numberplates on hire cars start with a Z, which can make them a target for thieves, so keep valuables hidden and remove them when the car is unattended. Hire cars can be taken from South to North Cyprus for the day, but check first that this does not invalidate your insurance. Goods purchased in the North may be confiscated at the checkpoint on returning to the South.

Driving conditions

Place names are usually given in both Greek and English, but signposting can be erratic so a map is a good idea. Major roads, including motorways, are well surfaced but minor roads can be rough and heavily potholed. All speed limits are posted in kilometres per hour. On entering a built-up area the speed limit automatically drops to 50km/h, and this is indicated by the sign marked *Katikómi Periokhî*.

North Cyprus

Roads here tend to be less well maintained. Speed limits are the same as in the South. Signs are mostly in English. Take care when driving around military vehicles, and keep clear of the buffer zone either side of the Atilla Line.

FACT FILE CYPRUS

Speed limits	Urban	Open road	Motorway
Car	50km/h	80km/h	100km/h
Towing	50km/h	80km/h	100km/h
Traffic regulations			
Essential equipment	Warning triangle		
Minimum driving age	18yrs		
Drink-drive limit	90mg alcohol per 100ml blood		
Child in front seat	Minimum 5yrs		
Seat belts	Compulsory in front and rear seats		
Motorcyclists	Must wear a crash helmet and use headlamp at all times		
Emergency telephone numbers			
Police/fire/ambulance	112 or 199		

Hiring a car is a good way to explore the picturesque countryside of Cyprus

TURKEY

Although not strictly part of Europe, Turkey is included here because many holidaymakers like to rent a hire car there just as they would in any other Mediterranean resort. A hire car opens up great possibilities of exploring this vast country. Anyone interested in seeing historic sites will appreciate having the flexibility to visit some of the most spectacular ruins off the main excursion routes.

Defensive driving

Driving in Turkey is not for the faint-hearted. Speeds are high, caution low and overtaking manoeuvres performed at the narrowest opportunity. It's vital to drive defensively, creating space around your vehicle to allow for the antics of other drivers. Roads are mostly in fair condition but be careful of potholes causing other traffic to swerve without warning. Avoid driving at night (local traffic may be poorly lit) and in wet weather (rain on oily roads forms a lethal cocktail). Avoid the major cities, especially Istanbul and Ankara where driving is at its most chaotic.

Toll motorways are being introduced and these offer a good value and easier alternative to more hectic local roads. If you are involved in an accident it is illegal to move any of the vehicles involved before the police arrive. You must carry two warning triangles, one to place in front of an immobilised vehicle and one behind it. Police can impose on-the-spot fines.

Many of Turkey's fascinating ancient ruins are hard to visit unless you have your own transport

FACT FILE TURKEY

Speed limits	Urban	Open road	Motorway
Car	50km/h	90km/h	120km/h
Towing	40km/h	70km/h	80km/h
Traffic regulations			
Essential equipment	Two warning triangles, first aid kit, fire extinguisher		
Minimum driving age	17yrs		
Drink-drive limit	50mg alcohol per 100ml blood		
Child in front seat	Minimum 12 years		
Seat belts	Compulsory in front seats		
Motorcyclists	Must wear a crash helmet		
Emergency telephone numbers			
Police	155		
Fire	110		
Ambulance	112		
Useful phrases			
Bozuk satıh	Rough surface		
Dikkat	Attention		
Dur	Stop		
Park yapılmaz	No parking		
Tamirat	Roadworks		
Giremez	No entry		
Tek yön	One way		
Yavaş	Slow		
Yaya geçidi	Pedestrian crossing		
Yol kapalı	Road closed		

DRIVING IN
EASTERN
EUROPE

Since the fall of the Berlin Wall and the collapse of communism in Europe, British motorists have faced the enticing alternative of pointing their vehicle eastwards after crossing the Channel instead of following a traditional holiday route to southern France, Italy or Spain.

183

The entrance of the Baltic states (Estonia, Latvia and Lithuania) into the EU gives a further incentive to explore this fascinating region. But be prepared for some challenging driving conditions. Cash for road maintenance has not been abundant in some areas so road surfaces can be rough. Local vehicles also tend to be older and less well maintained, as well as sometimes poorly lit at night.

Standard European road signs are used throughout the region, but the further east you go, the more likely you are to encounter unusual motoring laws. Areas of the Balkans remain risky to travel in so consult the latest advice from the foreign office before you leave.

Driving further east into Russia and neighbouring countries is recommended for experienced travellers only. Although potentially rewarding, road conditions in these countries can be poor, crime levels high and bureaucracy tortuous if you run into trouble.

Elderly Skodas are a familiar sight throughout Eastern Europe

POLAND

Poland is constructing a new motorway system but existing single carriageway major routes can be busy and sometimes in poor repair. As is usual in Eastern Europe, traffic coming from the right has priority. In deference to the harsh winters, from October to February dipped headlamps must be used by day as well as night. Use headlamps to signal when you intend to overtake. Do not drink anything at all before driving. Police are authorised to collect on-the-spot fines. Car crime is a serious problem in Poland, so always leave your car in a guarded car park. There have been cases of gangs posing as police holding up vehicles with foreign number plates, particularly in tourist areas such as the Polish lake district.

FACT FILE POLAND

Speed limits	Urban	Open road	Motorway
Car	60km/h	90-110km/h	130km/h
Towing	60km/h	80km/h	80km/h
Traffic regulations			
Essential equipment	Warning triangle		
Minimum driving age	18yrs		
Drink-drive limit	20mg alcohol per 100ml blood		
Child in front seat	Minimum 10yrs unless using a child restraint		
Seat belts	Compulsory in front and rear seats		
Motorcyclists	Must wear a crash helmet and use headlamp at all times		
Emergency telephone numbers			
Police	997		
Fire	998		
Ambulance	999		
Useful phrases			
Wstęp wzbroniony	No entry		
Wyjście	Exit		

CROATIA

Tourists are enthusiastically rediscovering Croatia, which combines beautiful coastal scenery with a rugged mountainous interior. Winter conditions in the mountains can be severe so winter tyres or snow chains may be required. Roads are generally well maintained but they can become heavily congested at busy periods along the coast, and queues can form at border crossings. Some motorways, bridges and tunnels have tolls. Cars towing a trailer or caravan must carry two warning triangles. It is illegal to overtake military convoys. The police are empowered to impose on-the-spot fines. If entering Croatia with a damaged car you should obtain a certificate for the damage at the border.

FACT FILE CROATIA

Speed limits	Urban	Open road	Motorway
Car	50km/h	80-100km/h	130km/h
Towing	50km/h	80km/h	80km/h
Traffic regulations			
Essential equipment	Warning triangle, spare bulbs, first aid kit, reflective jacket		
Minimum driving age	18yrs		
Drink-drive limit	50mg alcohol per 100ml blood		
Child in front seat	Minimum 12yrs		
Seat belts	Compulsory in front and rear seats		
Motorcyclists	Must wear a crash helmet and use headlamp at all times		
Emergency telephone numbers			
Police	92		
Fire	93		
Ambulance	94		
Useful phrases			
Osiguranje	Insurance		
Ulaz zabranjen	No entry		

CZECH REPUBLIC

Most visitors to the Czech Republic head straight for Prague, but the rest of the country – a beautiful mix of mountains, lakes, spa towns and castles – repays closer investigation by car. To use the motorway network you must display a vignette which can be purchased at the border. Do not drink any alcohol at all before driving. Use dipped headlamps at all times during the winter months. Give way to buses and trams. Take care at level crossings, which often have no barrier, and keep to 30km/h when approaching them. Accidents causing injury or more than minor damage must be reported to the police, who can collect on-the-spot fines.

FACT FILE CZECH REPUBLIC

Speed limits	Urban	Open road	Motorway
Car	50km/h	90km/h	130km/h
Towing	50km/h	80km/h	80km/h
Motorcycle	50km/h	90km/h	90km/h
Traffic regulations			
Essential equipment	Warning triangle, spare bulbs, first aid kit		
Minimum driving age	18yrs		
Drink-drive limit	Zero alcohol per 100ml blood		
Child in front seat	Minimum 12yrs/1.5m		
Seat belts	Compulsory in front and rear seats		
Motorcyclists	Must wear a crash helmet and use headlamp at all times		
Emergency telephone numbers			
Police	158		
Fire	150		
Ambulance	155		
Useful phrases			
Jednosměrný provoz	One way		
Zákaz parkování	No parking		

HUNGARY

Hungary has a mostly well-maintained road system including motorways, some of which are toll roads. Dipped headlamps must be used at all times outside built-up areas. Main beam should not be used when driving in town, and the horn is not permitted in town except in an emergency. Look out for horse-drawn carts in rural areas, especially after dark when they may be unlit. If your car sustains damaged bodywork you must obtain a certificate from the police. Carrying fuel in a can is not permitted. Do not drink any alcohol at all before driving. Always give way to trams and buses at junctions and when they are pulling out from the kerb, and pass railway crossings at a walking pace. Vehicles left in a no-parking zone will be removed.

FACT FILE HUNGARY

Speed limits	Urban	Open road	Motorway
Car	50km/h	90-110km/h	130km/h
Towing	50km/h	70km/h	80km/h
Traffic regulations			
Essential equipment	Warning triangle, first aid kit, reflective jacket		
Minimum driving age	18yrs		
Drink-drive limit	Zero alcohol per 100ml blood		
Child in front seat	Minimum 12yrs/1.5m		
Seat belts	Compulsory in front at all times and in rear outside towns		
Motorcyclists	Must wear a crash helmet and use headlamp at all times		
Emergency telephone numbers			
Police	107		
Fire	105		
Ambulance	104		
Useful phrases			
Egyirányú	One way		
Parkolás tiros	No parking		

BULGARIA

Western tourists are starting to discover the attractions of Bulgaria's Black Sea resorts, as well the fine skiing available in the Rila mountains. However, driving conditions here are suitable for more adventurous motorists only. At the border you must pay an entry fee and have your car's wheels disinfected. Car crime is rife with instances of carjacking at night and thieves posing as police. if your car is stolen in Bulgaria you will be liable for import duty on it and you should take out insurance to cover this. Accidents must be reported to the police and the resulting bureaucracy can be tortuous. Although the new toll motorways are well surfaced, other roads can be rough. Unlit farm carts and animals are a hazard at night. Filling stations can be infrequent in rural areas, and it's best to stick to multinational brands to ensure quality. Road signs are in Roman as well as Cyrillic alphabets.

FACT FILE BULGARIA

Speed limits	Urban	Open road	Motorway
Car	50km/h	90km/h	120km/h
Towing	50km/h	70km/h	100km/h
Traffic regulations			
Essential equipment	Warning triangle, first aid kit, fire extinguisher		
Minimum driving age	18yrs		
Drink-drive limit	50mg alcohol per 100ml blood		
Child in front seat	Minimum 12yrs		
Seat belts	Compulsory in front seats		
Motorcyclists	Must wear a crash helmet		
Emergency telephone numbers			
Police	165/166		
Fire	160		
Ambulance	150		

ESTONIA

Estonia has been more successful than many of the old Socialist Republics of the Soviet Union in making the transition from communism to western capitalism, and the country has a strong Scandinavian atmosphere. Attractions range from Tallinn's picturesque old town to the unspoiled Lahemaa national park. Driving in Estonia is straightforward, but take all possible security measures as car crime is a problem. Headlights must be lit at all times, and winter tyres must be fitted from October to April. Don't drink at all when driving as there is a zero limit. Speed limits are increased on certain roads from 90km/h to 110 or 120km/h during the summer months, but drivers who have held their licence for less than two years must keep below 90km/h at all times. When parking in larger towns you need to display a ticket which is available from local vendors.

FACT FILE ESTONIA

Speed limits	Urban	Open road	Motorway
Car	50km/h	90-110km/h	-
Towing	50km/h	90km/h	-
Traffic regulations			
Essential equipment	Warning triangle, first aid kit, fire extinguisher, wheel chocks		
Minimum driving age	18yrs		
Drink-drive limit	Zero alcohol per 100ml blood		
Child in front seat	Small children must be in restraint		
Seat belts	Compulsory in front and rear seats		
Motorcyclists	Must wear a crash helmet and use headlamp at all times		
Emergency telephone numbers			
Police	110		
Ambulance/fire	112		
Breakdown assistance	1888		

LATVIA

Latvia's attractions are well worth exploring by car; these include some beautiful coastal towns and beaches, the caves and castles of the Gauja valley and the cosmopolitan capital Rīga. Main roads are generally well maintained and traffic is light (car ownership in Latvia is among the lowest in Europe). However, driving in Rīga can be hectic so it's best to find a secure parking place there and switch to public transport. Some rural roads are unsurfaced so take extra care on them (see the advice on p118). Headlights must be lit at all times and drivers who have held their licence for less than two years must not exceed 80km/h. Winter conditions can be severe. If your car is involved in an accident do not attempt to move it until the police give permission, even if it is blocking the road. A British driving licence is valid for visits of up to six months.

FACT FILE LATVIA

Speed limits	Urban	Open road	Motorway
Car	50km/h	90km/h	90-100km/h
Towing	50km/h	90km/h	90-100km/h
Traffic regulations			
Essential equipment	Warning triangle, first aid kit, fire extinguisher, spare light bulbs		
Minimum driving age	18yrs		
Drink-drive limit	50mg alcohol per 100ml blood		
Child in front seat	Minimum 12yrs/1.5m unless using restraint		
Seat belts	Compulsory in front and rear seats		
Motorcyclists	Must wear a crash helmet and use headlamp at all times		
Emergency telephone numbers			
Police	02 or 112		
Fire	01		
Ambulance	03 or 112		

LITHUANIA

A land of scenic lakes and forests, with a spectacularly attractive capital Vilnius, Lithuania has a long and individual history and it was the first Baltic state to break away from the USSR. Delays have traditionally been common for motorists entering the country at border crossing points with Poland, but the entry of both these countries into the EU in May 2004 should hopefully ease problems here. Headlights must be used day and night at the beginning of the school year in September, and from November to March. Winter conditions can be severe in Lithuania so equip your car accordingly. In summer some motorway speed limits are raised from 110 to 130km/h. Car crime is a serious problem; in larger towns you should use guarded car parks, especially when leaving your car overnight. Police are authorised to impose on-the-spot fines.

FACT FILE LITHUANIA

Speed limits	Urban	Open road	Motorway
Car	50km/h	90-100km/h	110-130km/h
Towing	50km/h	90km/h	90km/h
Traffic regulations			
Essential equipment	Warning triangle, first aid kit, fire extinguisher		
Minimum driving age	18yrs		
Drink-drive limit	40mg alcohol per 100ml blood		
Child in front seat	Minimum 12yrs unless using restraint		
Seat belts	Compulsory in front and rear seats		
Motorcyclists	Must wear a crash helmet		
Emergency telephone numbers			
Police	02		
Fire	01		
Ambulance	03		

SLOVAKIA

Visitors heading for Slovakia's Tatra mountains should prepare for alpine driving conditions. A vignette (*nálepka*) is needed to drive on the motorways and certain major highways. This is available at borders and valid for one year. Check before trying to use certain border crossings which can be restricted to locals only. Do not drink any alcohol at all before driving. Always give way to a tram pulling out, or signalling a right turn. Use dipped headlamps at all times. Report any damage caused to your car in an accident to the police, or you may run into difficulties when leaving the country. Police can impose on-the-spot fines.

FACT FILE SLOVAKIA

Speed limits	Urban	Open road	Motorway
Car	50km/h	90km/h	130km/h
Towing	50km/h	80km/h	80km/h
Motorcycle	50km/h	90km/h	90km/h
Traffic regulations			
Essential equipment	Warning triangle, spare bulbs, first aid kit		
Minimum driving age	18yrs		
Drink-drive limit	Zero alcohol per 100ml blood		
Child in front seat	Minimum 12yrs/1.5m		
Seat belts	Compulsory in front and rear seats		
Motorcyclists	Must wear a crash helmet and use headlamp at all times		
Emergency telephone numbers			
Police	158		
Fire	150		
Ambulance	155		
Useful phrases			
Zákaz parkovania	No parking		
Zákaz vjazdu	No entry		

SLOVENIA

Slovenia has many attractions, including mountains and beaches, and its picturesque capital, Ljubljana. Traffic can be heavy and the motorway network is currently being extended; tolls are payable on motorways. Headlamps must be lit at all times. In alpine areas gradients are steep and winter weather severe. The 'give way to the right' rule applies, even on roundabouts where traffic entering has priority. Do not overtake a school bus when stopped. Not all petrol stations accept credit cards, and importing petrol in a spare can is not permitted. When parking in town you may need to purchase a coupon from a ticket machine or local vendor. Police are authorised to impose on-the-spot fines.

FACT FILE SLOVENIA

Speed limits	Urban	Open road	Motorway
Car	50km/h	100km/h	130km/h
Towing	50km/h	100km/h	100km/h
Traffic regulations			
Essential equipment	Warning triangle, spare bulbs, first aid kit		
Minimum driving age	18yrs		
Drink-drive limit	50mg alcohol per 100ml blood		
Child in front seat	Minimum 12yrs		
Seat belts	Compulsory in front and rear seats		
Motorcyclists	Must wear a crash helmet and use headlamp at all times		
Emergency telephone numbers			
Police	113		
Fire	112		
Ambulance	112		
Useful phrases			
Brezplacno	Free parking		
Placilno Parkirnine	Parking fee payable		

DRIVING IN NORTH AMERICA

North America is a hugely popular destination for British motorists. Hiring a car is an ideal way to see both the United States and Canada, and fly-hire deals are competitively priced and easy to arrange from the UK. Motorhomes are also available for hire.

Distances are vast by European standards – Arizona alone is nearly twice the size of England and Wales – so it's important not to set yourself too ambitious a schedule. However, roads are excellent and lightly trafficked out of the major conurbations, and cheap fuel (about a third of European prices) makes covering long distances surprisingly economical.

Do check you have adequate insurance cover when hiring a car. Americans are famously litigious and claims for damages can dramatically inflate the cost of an accident. Liability cover, which insures you against claims made by a third party, is vital – make sure you get at least $1m of cover.

Hiring a vehicle is the best way to explore America's wide open spaces; cheap fuel means driving there is economical too

UNITED STATES

Big country
"One of the most striking features of American driving is that of distance. Driving from Boston in the north-east to Los Angeles in the south-west would cover somewhere around 4,000 miles. Whilst distances are measured in miles, in conversation your journey will invariably be measured in driving hours. Thus, you can expect to hear that your motel is five hours away and not 250 miles"
Jane Simkins

Life in North America revolves around the car. Most people drive to get anywhere, even if it's just a couple of blocks down the road. Cars are larger than we're used to in Europe, although enormous 'Yank tank' sedans are giving way to off-roaders, people carriers and pick-ups. Don't be concerned about hiring a large car in the US, as roads and parking spaces are all big enough to match.

Driving habits
Almost everyone drives an automatic car, which adds to the relaxed driving atmosphere in most of the US, as do low *freeway* (motorway) speed limits. For years these were set at 55mph, but most states have now raised their limits to 65 or 70mph.

American driving sometimes seems lax by European standards, although outside the big cities American drivers tend to be lazy not aggressive. Beware of drivers who turn or change lanes without bothering to signal. Confusingly, a car's rear indicator, or *turn signal*, is normally a flashing red brake light, not a separate yellow indicator light. Overtaking is permitted in any lane on the freeway.

Americans may speak English but motorists will need to learn a whole new language all the same.

DRIVING IN NORTH **AMERICA**

Your *auto* has a *hood* not a bonnet and a *trunk* not a boot. You fill it with *gas* not petrol, it has a *windshield* not a windscreen and *tires* not tyres.

Highway rules vary considerably between states. Get advice when you hire a car about local speed limits, parking regulations and other unusual rules. Road signs vary between states too, although US signs are easy to understand because they are usually given as a written message rather than a pictogram.

Direction signposting can be poor, so make sure you have a good map. Directions at junctions often give road number and compass heading (North, South, East, West), so make a note of the road numbers you need to take before setting off. Watch out for Interstate highways that confusingly have a different local reference number.

In most US states right turns are allowed at red traffic lights unless there is a sign stating otherwise. You must first come to a complete halt and ensure the road is clear before proceeding.

At multiple junctions, the driver who arrives at the junction first has priority. If two or more cars arrive at once, give way to the right. Always stop for a school bus that is stationary with its lights flashing.

 Give way

 Pedestrians crossing

 Speed limit for freeway exit ramp

 Railroad crossing

 Interstate highway marker

America has a vast network of freeways, although speed limits are often lower than in Europe

Road to ruin
"Some city streets, for example in New York, are notoriously potholed and covered with metal plates. Local motorists reportedly have to pay an extra $150 per annum for repairs to suspensions as a result."
Gareth Zimmerman

Congestion
Urban freeways commonly have a High Occupancy Vehicle (HOV) lane. At certain times of day this lane is reserved for cars with the posted minimum number of occupants in an effort to encourage car sharing and cut congestion. In busy conditions traffic usually flows more quickly in this lane. Fines for using it illegally can be high.

Parking
Regulations vary, but painted kerbs usually indicate that parking restrictions are in force. In California, for instance, a white-painted kerb means you can stop to let out or pick up a passenger; yellow means you can stop briefly for deliveries; green allows parking for a specified time; blue indicates disabled only parking; and red means no parking or stopping at any time. Always park in the direction of traffic flow, and don't park within 15ft of a fire hydrant.

Drink-driving
The drink-drive limit in most US states is the same as in the UK, at 80mg alcohol per 100ml of blood, and drink-driving is a serious offence. Drivers aged under 21 are not permitted to drink any alcohol at all before driving. In most states it is against the law to carry an open bottle of alcoholic drink inside the car unless it is shut away in the boot.

Gas stations
When buying fuel in the US, many gas stations require you to pay before you start pumping. If you fill up for less than the amount you've paid for, return to the cashier to collect your change. Fuel is sold by the gallon, but it's the US gallon, equivalent to 3.8 litres, not the 4.6-litre imperial gallon. Don't pull in at a full-service pump unless you specifically want an attendant to fill your tank, check your oil and clean your windshield, as you pay significantly more per gallon for the privilege. Three grades of octane are available. Most hire cars are happy with the cheapest grade, but check with your rental company to be certain.

FACT FILE UNITED STATES*

Speed limits	Urban	Open road	Motorway
Car	30mph	65mph	70mph
Towing	30mph	65mph	70mph
Traffic regulations			
Minimum driving age	16yrs		
Drink-drive limit	80mg alcohol per 100ml blood (zero for under 21yrs)		
Child in front seat	Minimum 4yrs unless using a child restraint		
Seat belts	Compulsory in front and rear seats		
Motorcyclists	Riders and passengers under 21yrs must wear a crash helmet and headlamp must be used at all times		
Emergency telephone numbers			
Police	911		
Fire	911		
Ambulance	911		
*Applies to Florida. Regulations may differ in other states			

Everything seems bigger in America: some RVs (the US term for motorhomes) are so vast that owners tow their everyday transport along behind

CANADA

Serious hazard – detour if necessary

No overtaking

Unsurfaced road ahead

School zone: speed limit applies 8am to 5pm on school days

Playground zone: speed limit applies dawn to dusk every day

Driving in Canada is generally similar to driving in America, except in French-speaking Quebec where it can feel remarkably like driving in France. Distances are measured in kilometres and not miles as in the US. Fuel is a little more expensive than south of the border, but it's still cheap by UK standards.

Traffic rules

Many Canadian provinces require dipped headlamps to be used in the daytime as well as at night. Right turns are allowed at red traffic lights after stopping to check it's safe, everywhere except in Quebec.

At multiple junctions, the vehicle that arrived first has right of way. Look out for pedestrians too: in Canada they have right of way at all intersections without stop lights.

Don't overtake a school bus with flashing red lights. Passing with caution is allowed when the bus displays flashing amber lights immediately before and after coming to a halt. In school zones, a speed limit of 30kph may apply during school hours.

Parking

A green circle containing the letter P means it's fine to park during the hours indicated; a red circle with the P crossed out means parking is prohibited.

Car hire

Rental companies normally permit drivers to cross the border from America to Canada and vice versa. Border formalities are generally brief, although queues can form at busy periods.

Wildlife

Always be on the alert for animals crossing the road in front of you, especially moose in forested areas. Canadian winters are harsh, so take sensible precautions when setting out in icy conditions and heed local weather warnings.

FACT FILE CANADA*

Speed limits	Urban	Open road	Motorway
Car	50km/h	80km/h	100km/h
Towing	50km/h	80km/h	100km/h
Traffic regulations			
Minimum driving age	16yrs		
Drink-drive limit	50mg alcohol per 100ml blood		
Child in front seat	Minimum weight 18kg unless using a child restraint		
Seat belts	Compulsory in front and rear seats		
Motorcyclists	Must wear a crash helmet and use headlamp at all times		
Emergency telephone numbers			
Police	911		
Fire	911		
Ambulance	911		

Applies to British Columbia. Regulations may differ in other provinces

Canada's wildlife is a great attraction for visitors – but wandering moose can be a serious hazard on the road

DRIVING IN
AUSTRALASIA

Hiring a car is a great way to explore the spectacular open spaces of Australia and New Zealand. Distances between sights can be long but once out of the major towns traffic is usually light.

For visitors from the UK driving down under provides few surprises – especially as traffic in both countries drives on the left side of the road.

Because of the low population density motorways only run around larger urban centres. Main highways connecting towns are usually well-maintained single carriageway roads, but you don't have to venture far off the main routes to encounter gravel roads. Most are in good shape, but bear in mind that your hire car insurance may not cover you off the tarmac.

Drivers down under tend to be laid back rather than aggressive, especially in rural areas. Animals may be a bigger problem on the road in country areas – kangaroos in Australia, sheep in New Zealand.

There are some spectacular sights to enjoy down under, both natural and – like Sydney's Opera House – man-made

AUSTRALIA

Beware of kangaroos

Roundabout ahead

Beware – slow-moving vehicles entering

Stop sign ahead

Reserved for cars with three or more occupants at times shown

Away from its major cities Australia has vast, empty stretches of wild country. Outback Australia is magnificent to drive through but distances are huge so don't be over-ambitious when planning your itinerary and take frequent breaks to guard against fatigue. Even Melbourne and Sydney, which look so close on the map, are a 550-mile drive apart. If you're planning a big trip, consider hiring cars separately in areas you want to explore and travel between them by plane or train. Motorhomes are becoming easier to hire, though are less popular than you might expect; most tourists stick to a car and spend the nights in the good value motels that abound across Australia.

Driving conditions
Roads between cities are generally two-lane only. There are usually overtaking lanes at regular intervals, generally at ascents which slow trucks, and these are signposted some distance in advance.

Outback tracks
For a really spectacular drive, tackle an Outback track. A few of these are suitable for a conventional two-wheel-drive car but always take local advice before setting out. Four-wheel-drive vehicles are also available for hire. Remember that when things go wrong in the Outback, disaster can follow quickly, so prepare thoroughly for your trip and stay within the limits of your experience. Tell someone your route and destination and ask them to notify the police if you have not contacted them by an agreed time. Permits are needed to pass through most Aboriginal land, and also to visit some national parks.

Bad weather
Seasonal rainfall can quickly wash out a track and make it impassable. Roads may be closed in the wet season even to four-wheel-drive vehicles to avoid them churning up the surface which, when dry, forms impassable ruts. Fines for drivers using a road that's officially closed can be severe.

AUSTRALASIA

Speed limits

A general speed limit of 60km/h applies in built-up areas but lower limits – down to 10km/h in a shared traffic zone – may be posted. Speeding and drink-driving are severely dealt with in Australia and police make extensive use of radar to enforce speed limits. Try speeding in the state of Victoria and you will certainly be caught and fined. Until recently the Northern Territory was one of the few places in the world without speed limits; however, a limit of 130km/h has now been imposed on main highways across the Territory, and a 110km/h limit on other rural roads.

Animals

Cattle and kangaroos are a major hazard on country roads. A collision with a heavy creature like this can be serious, and further accidents are caused by drivers swerving to avoid an animal. Local cars are often fitted with roo bars to lessen the impact but hire cars usually aren't. Avoid driving at night, and take great care around dawn and dusk when animals are most active.

Ayers Rock (Uluru) is in the heart of the Outback but is easily accessible by paved highway

AUSTRALIA

Traffic priorities

The give way to the right rule applies. In built-up areas priorities are usually clearly marked, but on rural roads with no markings be ready to yield priority to vehicles entering from the right. Rural roads are often single track. Pull off the road to let oncoming traffic pass – if you simply pull on to the gravel at the side of the road and keep driving you risk getting a cracked windscreen from flying stones. In more remote areas, it's customary and polite to acknowledge drivers you meet with a wave of the hand. Pull well over and slow down if you see a road train coming. These 50-metre long monster trucks can kick up a blinding plume of dust.

Don't drive with your arm (or any other part of your body) hanging out of the window – it's an offence in the Northern Territory.

Parking

Always park in the direction of traffic flow. A no-standing sign means you may stop to let passengers on or off. There are parking meters in cities. Illegal parking will attract the attention of the local 'brown bombers' (parking wardens who, confusingly, wear grey uniforms).

Trams

Trams are a feature of driving in Melbourne. Only overtake a tram on the left, and stop behind at halts to allow passengers on and off. Obey road markings at right turns to avoid obstructing trams.

Fuel

Fuel is generally cheaper than in the UK, but prices can rise significantly in isolated areas. Fill up with fuel whenever you can in remote areas, especially before weekends when filling stations may close. If you're relying on getting fuel at an isolated filling station, phone ahead first to check it hasn't run out of supplies.

FACT FILE AUSTRALIA

Speed limits	Urban	Open road	Motorway
Car	60km/h	100km/h	110km/h
Towing	60km/h	100km/h	110km/h
Traffic regulations			
Minimum driving age	17yrs		
Drink-drive limit	50mg alcohol per 100ml blood (20mg for drivers under 25yrs who have held a licence for less than three years)		
Child in front seat	Minimum 12 months unless using a child restraint		
Seat belts	Compulsory in front and rear seats		
Motorcyclists	Must wear a crash helmet		
Emergency telephone numbers			
Police	000		
Fire	000		
Ambulance	000		

NEW ZEALAND

 Speed limit drops to 50kph in adverse conditions

 Gravel road ahead

 Give way to penguins

 Single lane bridge ahead: you have priority

 Railway crossing ahead

New Zealand's varied scenery and quiet roads provide a host of touring possibilities. Renting a motorhome is a popular option and makes a lot of sense as New Zealand is well provided with campsites, often in stunningly attractive situations. Check the insurance excess as this can be high for motorhomes, making it worthwhile paying extra to reduce it. On a tighter budget, it is possible to hire secondhand cars at cheaper rates, but again check the excess.

Road conditions

Traffic drives on the left but always be prepared to give way to the right. There are few motorways in New Zealand and the single carriageway main roads can be slow. The open road speed limit is 100km/h, but where a Limited Speed Zone (LSZ) is signposted this drops to 50km/h in adverse weather conditions. One peculiarity of New Zealand law is that when turning left into a side road, you must give way to an oncoming vehicle that wishes to turn across in front of your car into the same road. No left turn is allowed at a red traffic light except where a green filter arrow is lit. In town there are usually parking meters. Some cities have clearway zones and if you park in one illegally your car may be towed away.

Rural areas

Look out for sheep running loose in country areas. Unsealed minor roads are common so check whether your hire car insurance covers you when driving on them. The road often narrows to a single lane over bridges – a red arrow here means you have to give way. Take care at railway crossings as these may not be equipped with barriers. There's an occasional bridge shared by road and rail too, so look out for flashing lights which warn of an approaching train.

Car crime

Crime is generally low in New Zealand but there have been thefts from hire cars and motorhomes in tourist areas such as the Coromandel Peninsula and Queenstown, so take the usual precautions.

Driver's paradise
"The South Island really is a paradise. We were here three weeks before I overtook another vehicle, and in seven months I still have not seen or heard of a traffic jam."
Paul Fisher

FACT FILE NEW ZEALAND

Speed limits	Urban	Open road	Motorway
Car	50km/h	100km/h	100km/h
Towing	50km/h	80km/h	80km/h
Traffic regulations			
Minimum driving age	16yrs		
Drink-drive limit	80mg alcohol per 100ml blood (30mg for drivers under 20yrs)		
Child in front seat	Minimum 5yrs unless using a child restraint		
Seat belts	Compulsory in front and rear seats		
Motorcyclists	Must wear a crash helmet		
Emergency telephone numbers			
Police	111		
Fire	111		
Ambulance	111		

DRIVING IN SOUTHERN AFRICA

Southern Africa is an increasingly popular destination for fly-drive holidaymakers. Having the use of your own vehicle opens up whole new possibilities of seeing the region, which abounds with natural and cultural attractions including some of the worlds most spectacular game reserves.

Driving yourself allows you to take a more relaxed approach to the safari holiday. At National parks like Etosha in Namibia there are parking areas at water holes where you can sit in your car and quietly observe animals coming down to drink. It's a much less intrusive way of watching wildlife than in the big game parks of Kenya and Tanzania, where minibuses packed with tourists hurtle across the bush in pursuit of the 'big five' – lion, leopard, buffalo, elephant and rhino.

Traffic drives on the left which makes acclimatising to the roads here easier for British drivers. Roads in country areas are usually quiet and a pleasure to drive on, but less experienced drivers should steer clear of cities and busy main roads where driving styles can be intimidating. Many roads are gravel, which are generally a lot smoother to drive on they look and quite suitable for two-wheel-drive cars – but they do need to be treated with respect and tackled at reduced speeds.

Conditions on the road in Africa can be very different to what we're used to in the UK

SOUTH AFRICA

Sudden exit

"Unlike most express roads worldwide, freeways in South Africa do not have deceleration lanes when you exit them. Instead, on the approach to an exit, we have warning boards at 300, 200 and 100 metres. You must reduce your speed at these, as the off ramp invariably has a 90-degree bend just as you leave the freeway."
Jim Morrison

South Africa doesn't have the best reputation for safety, but as in many countries it's the cities that are the main problem. Avoid driving in Johannesburg or Cape Town, especially at night.

On country roads you are much less likely to run into trouble, but stay alert. Be wary about stopping if someone flags you down, or if you come across an accident in a lonely part of the bush. If in doubt carry on and alert the police at the next settlement. If you do stop keep your engine running, doors locked and windows closed until you are quite sure of the situation. Carrying a mobile phone (most UK models will work in South Africa) is a good idea.

Main roads are generally well maintained, but watch out for overcrowded minibuses and reckless overtaking. Local drivers expect slower traffic to move onto the hard shoulder to let them overtake, and sometimes expect oncoming vehicles to move over to make room for them too.

Regulations

As in the US, four-way intersections with stop signs are common in towns. The rule is that the first to arrive at the junction has priority. A single yellow line means no parking at any time; a single red line means no stopping. Don't park facing oncoming traffic. Report any accident involving another car to the police within 24 hours.

You may need cash at petrol stations which do not always accept credit cards. Some main highways, tunnels and bridges have tolls, but an alternative route is signposted where the toll begins.

Namibia

Namibia's traffic-free roads are ideal for a driving holiday. Many are gravel but still accessible by 2WD (see p118 for further advice). When driving to national parks check the gate closing times in advance. Keep to the speed limits in national parks – they are set low to avoid dust killing surrounding vegetation as well as to give you time to avoid animals on the road.

Robot ahead

If you're asking for directions in South Africa and someone tells you to turn left at the next robot, don't expect to find a Dalek standing at the street corner. 'Robot' just means traffic light

FACT FILE SOUTH AFRICA

Speed limits	Urban	Open road	Motorway
Car	60km/h	100km/h	120km/h
Towing	60km/h	100km/h	120km/h
Traffic regulations			
Minimum driving age	18yrs		
Drink-drive limit	50mg alcohol per 100ml blood		
Child in front seat	Minimum 12yrs		
Seat belts	Compulsory in front and rear seats		
Motorcyclists	Must wear a crash helmet		
Emergency telephone numbers			
Police	10111		
Ambulance	10117		

Copyright: South African Tourism

Hiring a car is the ideal way to enjoy South Africa's spectacular scenery

DRIVING FURTHER
AFIELD

Thirty years ago only the most adventurous holidaymakers ventured further than Spain or Greece. Nowadays the globe has opened up to tourists. India, Thailand, Africa and Central America are all popular destinations. And just as when visiting countries nearer home, it's tempting to broaden your horizons by hiring a car when you get there.

But driving is not necessarily as straightforward in more exotic regions as it is just over the Channel. Many developing countries have a poor driving safety culture and little enforcement of motoring regulations. Because of this accidents are frighteningly common. In Thailand the chance of a fatal accident is six times higher than in the UK; in India it's 13 times higher and in Kenya over 40 times higher. See page 94 for advice about how to stay safe when driving in the Third World.

If you are unfortunate enough to be involved in an accident then as a foreigner you are likely to get the blame regardless of the facts, and if you need medical treatment it may be of poor quality.

Even if you do survive the roads unscathed you may wish you had never bothered. Driving in Third World countries is nerve-wracking and stressful. You need to be on constant alert for unexpected behaviour, and even if they do not intend to be, local drivers can seem unpleasantly aggressive by western standards.

Driving in a busy city such as Bangkok is amazingly hectic and stressful: using public transport is usually a better option

Motorised rickshaws are a characterful sight on the streets of India

Asia

When driving in most Asian countries, there is at least the advantage that traffic drives on the left, as it does in the UK. **Thailand** is a popular destination where car hire is possible. Major international rental companies such as Hertz and Avis are represented; these may be a little more expensive than local outfits, but you're less likely to be caught out by small print in the rental contract. Thailand has 16,000km of national highways, mostly well maintained, but cluttered with carts, bicycles, animals and motorised rickshaws. Road signs usually have an English translation. Pavements marked with red and white stripes indicate no parking. Steer clear of Bangkok, which has some of the worst traffic jams on the planet. Military checkpoints are common in northern border areas so be prepared to stop unless you are waved through. Hiring a car with a driver can add surprisingly little to the overall cost and make the whole experience more pleasant.

Motorbike hire is popular at Thai resorts, as it is in **Goa**. Many tourists have come to grief riding motorbikes in these areas. Don't take the risk unless you are an experienced biker and make sure you take along your own helmet and protective gear.

India as a whole is one of the worst places in the world to drive. Roads are rough, traffic chaotic and the unofficial rule of the road is that the largest vehicle takes right of way. Much better to stick to

Animals on the road are an added hazard when driving in many Third World countries

India's incomparable rail network, which will take you most places a car can go and in a lot more safety and comfort.

Car hire is possible in **Indonesia**, but roads are crowded and dangerous. **China** has recently been experimenting with car rentals, but the stress of negotiating a sea of weaving bicycles is likely to drain any pleasure from the experience.

Japan is one Asian country where car hire can pay off, but only if you stay out of the cities as Japanese traffic congestion is notorious. Drivers there are polite and careful, drink-driving strictly prohibited, and speed limits low (40km/h in town, 80km/h on the motorway). Take expensive motorway tolls into account when budgeting your trip. Choose a small car that's easy to park, and take care when parking as some bays are designed to entrap your car if you overstay. Most Japanese road signs are in Roman script as well as Japanese, which makes them easier to decipher, but even so it can be a good idea to specify satellite navigation when you hire a car.

217

World of motoring

"In the Far East, two-wheeled transport comes into its own. Virtually everyone rides a motorcycle or is transported on one. In major cities traffic is congested and chaotic, and the flow of motorcycles is like a river running through the streets. This flow is relentless: riders do not usually stop and give way as we would in the west. There is continual merging of flow from the tributaries, or side roads, and those on the main road make allowance for this and reduce their speeds accordingly. If you do not go with the flow you are liable to be rammed from behind!"
Tim Dishman

Asian cities are notorious for their terrible traffic congestion

World of motoring
"Drive very carefully. You not only have to deal with other cars but also with crowds of pedestrians, cyclists, motorcyclists, carts and even animals. . . do not hesitate to sound your horn."
Moroccan National Tourist Office

Africa

Outside of Southern Africa (see p210-213), most African countries have such a terrible road safety record that driving in them cannot be recommended.

North Africa is a popular destination for British holidaymakers and hiring a car to explore the local area is straightforward there.

Tunisia has a well-maintained road network which includes a toll motorway running south from Tunis. However, few visitors drive because car hire here is expensive, and public transport, including cheap and convenient shared taxis – called *louages* – is usually a more cost-effective option. If you do decide to drive, look out for hitch hikers who turn out to be guides more interested in selling you something than getting to their destination. Driving is on the right, and as in Spain, to make a left turn you may have to first pull off the road to the right before crossing the main road. Gravel roads are common in the south so check your car hire insurance covers them.

Morocco has a minimum driving age of 21. There's a strict priority to the right rule, even at roundabouts. Take care at night when there are unlit mopeds, cycles, carts and animals on the road. If you are involved in an accident do not move the vehicles but wait for the police to arrive.

Not all African game parks are open to private cars, but those that are give a unique opportunity to view wildlife

Central and South America

Car hire is straightforward in much of Latin America, but the fast and furious pace of driving (and correspondingly high road casualty rate) in most countries is not conducive to a relaxing trip. Unless you have a lot of experience of driving in foreign countries, sticking to public transport is preferable. Many South American countries are notorious for armed highway robbery and police corruption, which makes driving in them an experience to avoid. Consult Foreign Office warnings (see p129) before hiring a car anywhere in South America.

A trip to **Mexico** can be an appealing option if you are driving in the southern United States, although few rental companies are happy about letting you cross the border in one of their cars. Only local motor insurance is recognised in Mexico anyway, making it essential to buy extra cover at the border. Taking a bus across and renting a car once you're there may be the easier option. Driving in Mexico is not for the faint hearted, although certain areas, such as the Baja California peninsula, provide excellent traffic-free driving through spectacular desert scenery. Toll roads are generally well maintained, and if you do break down the Mexican government has instituted teams of mechanics called *Angeles Verdes* (green angels) who patrol the major roads giving free help to tourists. On lesser roads watch out for pot holes and for *topes* – speed humps – when approaching towns and villages. Driving at night is not recommended due to cattle wandering on the road. Be cautious at all times and be on your guard for unusual driving habits. For instance it's usual for drivers to flash their *left* indicator to say its okay for you to overtake.

Driving is a little more relaxed in the **Caribbean** than in most of Central and South America, although road quality varies from good to terrible. Islands that were old British colonies (including the **Bahamas**) drive on the left, while those that were French or Dutch keep to the right and follow the usual give way to the right rule.

Even in the Arab world, road signs usually give an English translation as well

World of motoring
"In the Caribbean island of Nevis, look out for local youths in need of a lift who hop in and out of slow moving pick-ups at intersections. And you may encounter children playing games of cricket on the side roads – but remember that tiny Nevis has produced four West Indies test cricketers!"
Quentin Henderson

INDEX

223

AUTHOR'S **ACKNOWLEDGEMENTS**

224

The author would like to thank the following people for their help in supplying information used in this book: David Bridgen, David Clarke, Ian Ferguson, Mike Fourie, A F Frodsham CBE, Peter Gartside, AJ Goodwin, Mike Green, J Q Henderson, Astrid and Gunnel Ingham, Matt Littleson, John and Penny Mare, Birgitta Morris, Graeme Murray, Philip Reeve, Jane Simkins, Frank Smith, Eleanor Worthy, Gareth Zimmerman, Alexandra Metcalf, Beryl Dean, Bruce Harrison, Clare Reeves, David Gray, Derek Eastell, Des Lyver, Harry Wilby, Howard Prestage, Ivan Marner, Jim Fairclough, Jim Morrison, John Kent, Jonathan Sherwill, Les Spedding, Lyn Heslop, Mike Jobling, Paul Fisher, Peter Upton, R H Corbett, Rod Duggan, Wendy Furey, Andrew Jones, Ken Walsh, Tim Dishman, André Fontaine, Fiona Haig.